THE LETTERS OF
SAINT BONIFACE

TRANSLATED

WITH AN INTRODUCTION BY

EPHRAIM EMERTON

NEW YORK: MORNINGSIDE HEIGHTS

COLUMBIA UNIVERSITY PRESS

MCMXL

RECORDS OF CIVILIZATION
SOURCES AND STUDIES

EDITED UNDER THE AUSPICES OF THE
DEPARTMENT OF HISTORY, COLUMBIA UNIVERSITY

Foreword

A SHORT WHILE before his death Dr. Emerton turned over to me a manuscript comprising a translation of the correspondence of St. Boniface, upon which he had been at work during his last years. I then assured him that it would be printed in the "Records of Civilization," and he appeared happy in that assurance. Its publication now is a pious task long overdue, but conditions have been such that it was impossible to get it into print earlier.

Dr. Emerton recognized that the manuscript would need some revision by a competent scholar and expressed a desire to have the work done by Professor George La Piana. It is a pleasure here to record the readiness with which Professor La Piana gave of his time and of his broad scholarship in preparing the manuscript for the press and in reading the proofs.

In this work of editing both Professor La Piana and I felt that only the most necessary changes should be made. Dr. Emerton had his own canons in the translation of Latin texts. These have been honored, though in many places a more literal rendering might have seemed preferable. Many readers will probably feel that much fuller commentary on the many interesting and important points raised in the letters would have improved the volume and added to its usefulness; but since Dr. Emerton felt that little was to be gained by accompanying a translation with critical apparatus, preferring to let the letters speak for themselves, the editors have acquiesced in his known wishes in the matter. Editorial work has, therefore, consisted in some slight changes in the Introduction and such revision of the translation as seemed imperative. A brief bibliography has been added. The Columbia University Press has kindly provided the index.

A. P. E.

Montrose
June 1, 1940

INTRODUCTION

Boniface and the Frankish Church

THE WHOLE SUBJECT of foreign missions has recently been brought vividly before the American public by a volume with the arresting title *Re-thinking Missions*. The book is the report of a commission of laymen and clergymen, representing the most important Protestant denominations, which had spent two years upon the study of problems presented by existing conditions. The inquiry was prompted by grave doubts on the part of the friends and supporters of missions whether missionary efforts were being so wisely directed as to warrant further continuance, and whether any practicable changes of method would avail to restore confidence and stimulate renewed activity.

There could hardly be a more useful introduction to the correspondence of St. Boniface than this volume, twelve centuries later in time but singularly contemporaneous in the problems involved and in the suggestions for their solution. In both cases we have the impact of a civilization convinced of its own superiority upon another which it was bound to think of as inferior and which it felt obligated to elevate to higher levels of thought and action. In both cases the missionary motive was accompanied by a profound ignorance of the psychology of the "lower" peoples and by the contempt which ignorance is sure to beget. What we are accustomed to call the "missionary spirit" justified itself then as now by the undoubted fact that Christianity was from the beginning a missionary and exclusive religion. While other religious movements in the Roman melting pot of the first three centuries were mutually tolerant, Christianity refused to be absorbed into any kind of syncretism and fought its way through to final victory. In that attitude of exclusiveness it never wavered. Christianity was right, and hence all that was not Christian was wrong. Further, since persistent error implied moral turpitude, it was a part of the Christian duty not only to uplift but to punish the infidel with penalties in this life and in the life to come. On the other hand, the harshness of this judgment was mitigated, in the eighth as in the twentieth century, by the essential humanity of specially gifted leaders. Men differed then as now as to how the heathen were to be approached, and nowhere can this conflict of opinion be better studied than in the letters of this volume. Boniface was, first of all, an Anglo-Saxon, born and reared in the noble tradition of Pope Gregory the Great. He was the natural successor of the missionary Augustine, whose letters of inquiry addressed to Pope Gregory drew forth that remarkable series of instructions which might well serve as a wholesome corrective to the overzealous missionary of our own day. The great truth revealed to our generation by the comparative study of religion was spiritually foreshadowed in the thought of men like Gregory and Boniface. Spiritually, if not scientifically, they grasped the idea that the heathen gods were, after all, dim adumbrations of the one Divine Being, "ignorantly worshipped," whom they were declaring unto the heathen.

Our knowledge of the early life of Winfred, afterward called Boniface, is meager and uncertain. The biography by his pupil Willibald gives an obviously overdrawn picture of his precocious piety and intellectual endowment. It is the conventional "saint's life," subject to the necessary discount with which that type of literature must be treated. The date and place of his birth can be conjectured with some approach to accuracy. He was born probably on the border of the kingdom of Wessex in the neighborhood of Exeter and about the year 675. His family seems to have been prosperous and, judging from the social group with which he was identified, was probably of the lower nobility. Following the natural course for a bright boy of that day, he entered the monastery at Exeter at the age of seven (?) and remained there through his childhood, passing then to the abbey of Nursling in the diocese of Winchester and coming thus early under the influence of Bishop Daniel, with whom his relations continued to be intimate during his most active years. He appears to have been an eager student of the classics as well as of the Bible and the Fathers of the Church. After some years he was put in charge of the abbey school and, probably as soon as he reached the canonical age of thirty (c. 705), he was ordained priest. The way seemed open before him to the highest functions of the clerical life, but the missionary impulse was beginning to assert itself, and he was drawn irresistibly into the adventure which was attracting generous spirits in increasing numbers. The British Isles had received their culture and their religion from the Continent. Now, after a century and a half of assimilation and adjustment, they were prepared to repay the debt. During the generation before Winfred a double stream of missionary effort had been pouring across the Channel, carrying the Christian message to regions as yet scarcely touched by it. One branch of this stream had come from the Keltic side, the other from the Anglo-Saxon side of the island. Whatever may have been the origin of the Keltic Church, the one thing certain about it is that it was not Roman and that this distinction from the Anglo-Saxon was intensified into opposition by the racial conflict. The result was that two types of missionary foundations were transplanted to the Continent and flourished there until the Roman-Benedictine came definitely to supplant the earlier "British" forms of monastic life. It is probable that the distinction between the two has been unduly emphasized by modern writers. Upon points of doctrine there were no essential differences. In matters of form, such as the monastic tonsure and the date of the Easter festival, ancient controversies were perpetuated and served, as outward symbols are wont to do, to exaggerate otherwise unimportant rivalries. The analogy with the unhappy denominational futilities of modern missionary effort is obvious.

Our interest in this dual aspect of the missionary situation in the eighth century is that it gives us the outline of Winfred's activities throughout his whole career. We think of him primarily as the "Apostle to the Germans," meaning by this term the most important agent in the conversion of the North German tribes from paganism to Christianity. But conversion meant for him only a first step toward the organization and concentration of all Germanic Christendom under the leadership of Rome. In this latter effort his success was often endangered by the opposition of what he would have called in modern phrase "nominally Christian" communities, and there can be no reasonable doubt that these included the more or less active remnants of the earlier British foundations. Winfred himself was acutely conscious of his own Teutonic origin. His most intimate correspondents were the men and the women, high and low, with whom he spent the first forty years of his life. He lost no opportunity of utilizing the kinship of English and German to excite the sympathy of his people for the work of his mission. He did not even hesitate to lash their common vices, drunkenness and sensuality, with the scourge of his eloquence and to compare them unfavorably with the peoples of Frankland, Lombardy, and Rome. His love and loyalty for his own kinsfolk was one of the most evident motives of his reforming zeal.

The friends of Winfred seem to have used all their influence to keep him in England, and it was not until he was about forty years of age that he made his fateful decision. His first attack was directed at the most critical point, the low country of Frisia, where the Roman culture had been most obstinately resisted. Only one feeble outpost had been established at Utrecht, where another Anglo-Saxon, Willibrord, maintained an ineffectual episcopal see. A brief inspection convinced Winfred that his plan of campaign was premature. At all events, he soon abandoned it and returned to his place in England.

His purpose was unchanged, but his line of attack was to be different. Instead of direct action he began to employ the more prudent methods of diplomacy. It was now his first care to gain the support of Rome and then to make sure of help from the rising power of the Carolingian Mayors of the Palace. The greater part of a year was spent in Rome, where Pope Gregory II appears to have made careful inquiry into his personal qualities and the prospect of success for his mission. The result was a formal commission to the "devout priest Boniface" (No. IV) to carry the word of Christian truth to the "peoples still in the bonds of unbelief" as agent of the holy Apostle Peter and his successor, the bishop of Rome. The name Boniface, here used for the first time, henceforth replaces the Anglo-Saxon Winfred in all documents. No immediate results seem to have followed this first apostolic sanction. Leaving Rome and passing up through Lombardy, Boniface made his way in the summer of 719 to Bavaria and so on into Thuringia, at that time a long strip of territory stretching northward from the middle Danube to the middle Elbe, under nominal control of the Frankish kingdom and with scattered centers of Christian influence. Apparently this was rather a tour of inspection than serious missionary activity. Late in the year he turned westward to the Rhine and moved downstream once more to Frisia, where he was urged by Bishop Willibrord to stay as his assistant and eventual successor. Instead he turned southward into Hessen and remained there until 722, when, after making a preliminary report, he was called to Rome by Pope Gregory and there was consecrated bishop. His oath on this occasion (No. VIII) was a duplicate of that taken by the bishops of the Roman province, a confirmation of the close identification with Rome which is the keynote of all his future action. So far as possible he would conform to Roman instruction and Roman practice, but, as his letters show, he allowed himself a certain latitude in applying general principles to specific cases. Boniface now found himself in the peculiar position of a bishop with a large diocese possessing no fixed boundaries; he was entrusted with the task of gradually creating there an ecclesiastical province with its regular hierarchy, its dioceses, and its bishops. Only in regions where no precise diocesan limits had been fixed could such a roving commission be justified. It is clear proof of Boniface's zeal and ability that he proceeded as rapidly as circumstances permitted to the erection of bishoprics throughout the German lands eastward from the Rhine. Not, however, until the year 732, after the accession of Pope Gregory III and the installation of Boniface as archbishop, though still without a fixed seat, could this new development be realized.

In regard to the other side of Boniface's organizing work: his relations with the Frankish government were assisted by the world-

shaking events in and around this year 732. Pope Gregory II died
in 731. His successor, Gregory III, found himself in great danger
from the pressure of the unorthodox Lombards and was more
than anxious to stand well with the rising power of the Carolingian
Franks. On his side the Frankish leader, Charles Martel, needed
the moral support of Rome in the great struggle forced upon him
by the Moorish invasion of southern Gaul. The fate of Western
Christian civilization, decided on the plain of Poitiers in 732, involved the permanent alliance of Rome and Frankland, the two
main pillars of the Bonifatian edifice.

The condition of the Frankish Church under the later Merovin-
gian "good-for-nothings" was anything but encouraging. A complete episcopal and monastic organization was there, but it, too,
shared with the political structure the decline in spirit that was
dragging both toward an inevitable collapse. For more than two
generations there had been no gathering of the national Church
for deliberation or for common action. It was too much to expect
that Charles Martel would take any very active measures toward
recovery. Essentially a man of war and political action, he had
been, in relation to the Church, not hostile but certainly not indulgent. In his preparation for the campaign of 732 he had not
hesitated to make such demands upon the landed wealth of clerical
holders that he acquired the evil name of a despoiler of churches.
Urged to defend the Roman territory against the invading Lombards, he had steadily refused to embroil himself with an allied
people and had limited his interference to peaceful negotiations.

Toward Boniface Charles's attitude was much the same, not hostile but not very actively sympathetic. During the decade following the victory at Poitiers he was busily engaged in strengthening
his hold upon the surrounding Germanic peoples by whose aid
that decisive triumph had been made possible. Indirectly, therefore, he had been helping to consolidate the results of Boniface's
restless energy. His death in 741 left to his two sons, Pippin in the
West and Karlmann in the East, a legacy of established power
which each was to develop after his own fashion. Of the two,
Karlmann was of a temper distinctly more favorable to the pur-

poses of Boniface. Almost immediately Karlmann began negotiations for the calling of an assembly which, under the name of Concilium Germanicum (742), marks an epoch in the reconstruction of the Frankish Church. How far this new impulse was due to the initiative of the State and how far to that of Boniface has been the subject of rather violent controversy. On the one hand, it has been obviously in the interest of clerical historians to represent the whole movement as the outcome of the widespread Roman missionary effort of which Boniface was undoubtedly the guiding spirit. Viewed from this side, the Frankish State appears primarily as an auxiliary agent of the Roman power, indispensable to its success, but subordinate to its control. On the other hand, historians of the national development in the North have been especially interested to trace every indication of governmental influence in Church affairs. According to them the "princes" took the initial steps in reorganization. By the princes the reforming councils from 742 on were "called"; the acts of these Frankish assemblies were validated by their sanction; bishops were "appointed" by them; the property rights of churches were subject to their jurisdiction and were properly subordinated to the exigencies of public policy.

This is not the place for a detailed examination of these rival claims. The great historic truth underlying the secular conflict is that here were two forms of civilizing influence moving along together. Their normal lines of progress were parallel. In theory, each had its own resources and its own well-defined activities. In fact, these resources were confused by the working of economic law, and the lines of action crossed each other in a multitude of ways. It was to the interest of both Church and State that the functions of each should be more strictly defined. Assemblies which appear on the one side as "synods" were almost equally "diets," "Reichstage," "parliaments." Secular and religious affairs were mingled in the *acta*. It is interesting to note every indication of growing "nationalistic" tendencies, but the cautious historian must beware of using terms which became truly descriptive only after centuries of struggle. Nationalism in the modern sense was an almost unknown sentiment in the medieval scheme. The ghost of

Roman imperialism still walked in the imagination of capable and ambitious rulers of men; years before the death of Boniface, the man was born who was to give to this shadowy conception a form which, rising and falling, was to persist for a thousand years. And moving along with this empire of the sword was the empire of the spirit represented by the Roman papacy. Always in rivalry, frequently in bitter opposition, these two universal powers were united in a common hostility to the disintegrating tendencies of all those local movements which we class together as "nationalistic."

The guiding principle of Boniface's action during a whole generation was to keep himself in right relations with these two dominant powers in the western world. He needed the authorization of the papacy to give to his work the sanction of a divine command. He needed the physical support of the Frankish national government to provide the security without which his wide-flung missionary adventure would be impossible.

The Letters

THE DOMINANT NOTE throughout Boniface's letters is the success of the mission to which he vowed a life's devotion. All other interests are of importance only as they contribute to this one supreme purpose. Even his relation to Rome is to be judged from this point of view. Over and over again he declares his loyalty to the Roman system; but one feels that this was not so much an abstract sentiment as a necessary adjunct to successful missionary effort. Especially enlightening is the correspondence with Pope Zacharias (741–52). Boniface greets the new pope with all reverence and humility and begs for instruction in dealing with the perplexing problems of the Frankish reforms. Yet he does not hesitate to differ with the supreme pontiff on specific points and even goes so far as to insinuate that some of his greatest difficulties are due to the evil example of the Roman clergy (No. XL). He ventures to tell the pope of a report in Frankland that the papal

government has been involved in simoniacal dealings with Frankish clergy—a charge to which Zacharias makes an indignant but
not very effective reply (No. XLVI). It is interesting to compare
Boniface's relations to Rome and to the English Church. He desires instruction from Rome, but also from England. With Bishop
Daniel of Winchester he stands in the relation of fellow country-
man and pupil. He consults him on the best method of approach
to their heathen kinsmen and receives a long letter full of sound
common sense based upon the precepts of St. Augustine (No. LII).
One of the most remarkable letters is that in which Boniface, supported by five other bishops in Germany, also of Anglo-Saxon
origin, accuses King Ethelbald of Mercia of the foulest vices and
the most outrageous abuse of churches within his kingdom. The
summons to reform is supported from Scripture and even enforced
by the good example of heathen peoples, but there is no reference
to Rome, either as authority or as judge (No. LVII; cf. also Nos.
LVIII, LIX).

Boniface's attachment to his English connections is nowhere
more beautifully expressed than in a letter addressed to Abbot
Fulrad of St. Denis but obviously intended for King Pippin. Written probably in 752 and under the premonition of approaching
death, it commends his fellow workers, most of them Englishmen,
to the especial care of the king and begs him to ensure their welfare by appointing Boniface's colleague, the Englishman Lullus,
as eventual successor (No. LXXVI). Year after year we find the
record of gifts interchanged between the island and the Continent
—practical gifts of warm clothing and useful books sent out by
pious ladies from English convents (Nos. VII, XXII, XXVI) and
in return articles of luxury, pepper, spices, incense, myrrh, and
wine. King Ethelbert of Kent begs Boniface to send him an especially choice and well-trained pair of falcons (No. LXXXV), and
Boniface sends to the scapegrace King Ethelbald of Mercia "a
hawk and two falcons, two shields and two lances as a token of
true affection" (No. LV).

In matters of faith there can be no question of Boniface's complete orthodoxy. Upon specific details of ritual he was often

troubled by scruples which led him to seek advice from every available source—primarily, of course, from Rome, but also from colleagues of rank equal to his own. His function as a missionary bishop brought him face to face with several perplexing problems, the first with cases of baptism by unauthorized or heretical priests. How far should he go in accepting such baptisms and how far would he be justified in insisting upon the dangerous experiment of rebaptism? On the one hand was the risk of exposing a human soul to the peril of an invalid sacrament, and on the other the danger of casting doubts upon the validity of a sacrament once honestly performed and which, according to well-established precedent, could not be repeated. If the irregularity of the rite consisted in a verbal error, due perhaps to the ignorance of the officiating priest, ought this fact to be taken as a sufficient excuse? On all these points Boniface was inclined to take the liberal attitude, and on the whole he was well supported by his advisers and by the papal instructions. In no case do we see evidence of serious conflict (Nos. XVIII, LIV).

Still more difficult were the problems relating to marriage, especially in regard to the prohibited degrees of relationship. No other question seems to have lain so heavily upon Boniface's conscience. With all his desire to conform to the Roman standards, he evidently was puzzled. How could he make the heathen understand why they should not enter into a regular union with a relative in the fourth—not to say in the seventh—degree? And still worse, how to defend the prohibition of "spiritual" connections? One case is typical of the whole class of doubtful situations. A certain man had acted as godfather at a baptism. Later he had married the widowed mother of his godson. Should such a marriage be allowed? Acting on his general liberal principles, Boniface gave his approval; but his conscience was sorely troubled. His own knowledge of canon law did not cover the case, and we find him inquiring in every direction (Nos. XXIII, XXIV, XXV), but without reaching a unanimous opinion. "I cannot possibly understand," he writes to Archbishop Nothelm of Canterbury, "how, on the one hand, spiritual relationship in the case of matrimonial intercourse can be so great a sin, while, on the other hand, it is well established that by holy baptism we all become sons and daughters, brothers and sisters of Christ and the Church."

Another disturbing problem concerned the relations of the missionary with "false," "heretical," or "evil" priests. On no other point has there been so much or so heated controversy among students of Boniface. The letters are full of references to these irregular clergymen, but only in two or three cases do we have clear indications as to the precise nature of the offense. The society in which Boniface had to work was curiously compounded of Roman decadence and Teutonic barbarism, with the roughly organized Christian Church as the sole unifying and civilizing agency. The primal instincts of human nature would assert themselves against all restraints of a formal and largely alien culture. Individual chastity and monogamous marriage, with its requirement of unbroken fidelity on the part of both parties, were the indispensable requirements of a stable, orderly, and civilized society. As a Christian missionary Boniface was, of course, chiefly concerned with enforcing the Christian law as the motive power of social reform, but he was not indifferent to what we should call the "scientific" argument as well. In his denunciatory letter to King Ethelbald (No. LVII) he clinches his exhortations by pointing to the inevitable degeneracy of the English people as a result of laxity in their sexual relations.

The question as to how far Boniface might properly go in his intercourse with "evil" priests was especially trying whenever he was brought into direct relations with the Frankish court. He could not afford to offend the princes or their immediate attendants. Which was the lesser evil, to refuse all communication with the "sinful" clergy or to bear with them for the sake of the weaker brethren who were the special objects of his missionary efforts? His decision here was similar to those reached in other cases. The all-important thing was the welfare of the souls committed to his charge. His own position was secure. His manners were too well established to be corrupted by "evil communications." To withdraw himself from contact with the ungodly would seem to him a be-

trayal of trust, a desertion of those who looked to him for support
in their none too solid loyalty. So he was willing to hold communication with these doubtful priests in all except the most sacred
of Church functions. There he drew the line. In this matter he was
supported by the popes and by his friendly counsellors (Nos.
XVIII, LI, LII).

In making such concessions to human frailty Boniface excluded
all teachers of false doctrine. Two cases of obvious "heresy" are
of especial interest. Aldebert and Clemens were causing great confusion in Frankland by preaching extravagant doctrines and encouraging practices not authorized by canonical rule. Largely
through Boniface's activity their cases were brought before the
Roman synod of 745 and disposed of by papal authority. The detailed report in No. XLVII enables us to form an idea of the nature of their peculiar doctrines. Aldebert appears to belong in the
long and not dishonorable succession of "prophets" who, since men
began to think, have believed themselves to be specially inspired
vehicles of divine truth. Therein lay the burden of his offense.
It was not so much the fantastic decoration in which he clothed
his appeal to the people as it was the idea of individual, direct
inspiration that roused the spirit of Boniface. As agent of Roman
catholicism he could not tolerate that type of opposition. The case
of Clemens is even more puzzling. Of Keltic origin, he does not
seem to have been a representative of that Keltic missionary influence which Boniface was forced to combat. In some ways he suggests the type of early Protestantism. His main authority was the
Bible; he taught that marriage was the right and duty of the
Christian priest and preached the redemption of *all* souls, good
and evil, through the sacrifice of Christ. All this was obviously
hostile to the theory of one sole saving Church. We can perfectly
understand why Boniface threw himself into the campaign against
these "heretics" with all the energy of his nature. Through a
trusty agent he appeared at the Roman synod of 745 as prosecut-
ing attorney, and the sentence of condemnation was based primarily upon his presentation of the case.

Boniface's religious faith seems to have been notably free from that type of credulity covered rather vaguely by the word superstition. In denouncing heathen practices he is especially zealous against all kinds of incantation, witchcraft, soothsaying, and the like. He has respect for the value of historical evidence. How far he was willing to go in accepting a record of marvelous occurrences is shown in his report of one of those visits (which form so curious a chapter of medieval literature) of a disembodied soul to the place of departed spirits (No. II, cf. also No. XCII). Boniface writes to the abbess Eadburga the story told to him, "in the presence of three pious and most venerable brethren," by a certain monk of Wenlock in Shropshire. This monk, recovering from a violent fever, was taken out of his body and carried by a band of angels up to a height from which he could overlook the whole earth. There he was shown a vision of the Last Judgment and the warfare of good and evil spirits for the souls of men, including his own. Upon his return to the body, he told his story, and the report thereof became noised abroad, reaching the good lady Eadburga by the usual channels. She applies to her most trusted friend for a faithful version of the tale; but Boniface waits until he can fortify himself by a personal interview before witnesses and then tells the story as he heard it without comment. There is no reason to suppose that he was either more or less receptive to such marvels than his contemporaries. What he wished to be sure of was the sincerity of the reporter. The psychology of the phenomena reported did not concern him. He stood upon the same ground as the historian Bede, who reports precisely the same kind of psychic experiences with equally pragmatic calmness.

As to the technique of his missionary work Boniface gives us singularly little information. We should like to know in what language he addressed the unconverted Frisians and Saxons or the nominally Christian Franks and Bavarians. It is certain that two new languages, to be known as "German" and "French," were in process of formation. As an Anglo-Saxon, acutely conscious of his Teutonic kinship, he would, in all probability, have retained command at least of that dialect in which he had been reared. It is true, of course, that all his education had been based upon a reading

and speaking knowledge of Latin. Doubtless all his formal intercourse was conducted in Latin; but it is hard to believe that so
broadly human a nature should have lost the power to communicate freely with the people whom he especially desired to influence.
How are we to explain the stories of his preaching to throngs of
prospective converts if we suppose him to be using a language
which none of them could understand? The obvious answer would
be that, like John Eliot or his Jesuit rivals, he made use of inter-
preters, but of this there is no mention in the letters. More to the
point is the undoubted fact that to the untutored mind religion was
not so much a matter of individual conviction as of racial or tribal
property. Conversion depended, therefore, less upon persuasion
by oratorical appeal than upon the decision of tribal chieftains that
Christianity was a better investment than persistence in heathenism.
There is every indication that Boniface was keenly aware of this
fact and employed it effectively. In his own letters and in those of
successive popes, as well as in the edicts of Frankish princes, we
find abundant appeals to leaders high and low to bring their people
into the Christian fold. The motives in all such appeals are the
hope of reward and the fear of punishment in this world and the
next. We may fairly think of Boniface's public exhortations as
periodical encouragement to local effort. The most efficient supplement to the spoken word was the founding of churches or erection
of altars wherever a sufficient group of converts was gathered.
These were the nuclei around which a provincial organization could
be developed. It was a slow process, subject to frequent setbacks
due to the hostility of heathen neighbors or the lukewarmness of
half-Christianized leaders. As recruiting grounds for this service
monasteries were indispensable auxiliaries. As the frontier of Frank-
ish-Christian civilization was pushed forward to the north and east
the line of cloisters marched with it. Most notable of Boniface's
foundations was Fulda, the origins of which are clearly sketched in
the letters (Nos. LXX, LXXI, LXXIII). Fulda was to be forever
protected against encroachment from any power whatsoever by
the sole overlordship of Rome. Placed as it was in the midst of the
four peoples to whom Boniface had carried the word of God it was

to be his final resting place, a symbol of his unifying and civilizing work.

As to his personal quality, the unvarying ·evidence of the letters gives us the picture of a singularly even, well-balanced character. His dominant trait was gentleness, combined with an unflinching firmness when once his course of action was made clear. Making all allowance for extravagance in the expressions of affection on the part of his friends, we must still feel the force of a nature which could inspire such loyal devotion. In the whole range of his correspondence there is not a single note of suspicion or distrust. If in the early letters of Pope Gregory II there is a certain lack of cordiality, we have to consider that the volunteer missionary was under inspection and had to prove his quality still further before he could be sent out as the accredited agent of Rome. Such reserve was more than made up by the unstinted confidence of Gregory II in his later years and of his successors, Gregory III and Zacharias.

The physical equipment of Boniface must have been far removed from the anemic, ascetic type of the conventional monk. His continual journeys up and down the rough country called for courage and endurance that meant a vigorous and well-nourished body. He tells of his abstemious habits and it is only in his declining years that he complains of physical infirmities. However much of a prohibitionist he was for himself he was no kill-joy for others. He concludes a letter to Archbishop Egbert of York: ". . . we are sending you . . . two small casks of wine, asking you . . . to use it for a merry day with the brethren" (No. LXXV). The famous story of the Wuotan's oak may well serve as an illustration of his impetuous courage when the occasion called, and the final dramatic scene in his ill-starred Frisian expedition seems the logical climax to his strenuous life.

Altogether an engaging personality, the more appealing as one frees it from the mists of sainthood that have been thrown around it by the piety of succeeding ages and views it in the light of practical results. His is a broadly human figure, a man conscious of a great mission, conscious also of his own limitations and overcoming them by the power of an unconquerable faith.

Editions of the Letters

THE LETTERS OF BONIFACE were collected not long after his death (754/55) and are still extant in six different manuscripts. Of these three may be described as "originals" and may be briefly listed, as follows:

1. Munich, Staatsbibliothek, lat. 8112, transcribed at Mainz, probably in the latter part of the eighth, or early in the ninth, century.

2. Karlsruhe, Bädische Landesbibliothek, Rastatt 22, about 850, the work of several hands, revised in the eleventh century by Otloh of St. Emmeram. Written at Mainz, later used at Fulda.

3. Vienna, Nationalbibliothek, lat. 751. Also written at Mainz about 850 and later transferred to Cologne, perhaps about 870.

Manuscripts 4, 5, and 6 are probably—Tangl would say certainly—the work of Otloh, abbot of St. Emmeram in Bavaria, who, during a prolonged visit in Fulda (1062–66) collected materials for his life of Boniface.[1]

Fragmentary editions appeared in early collections, but the *editio princeps* of the whole correspondence of Boniface was that of Nikolaus Serarius, published at Mainz in 1605. This was followed by the edition of Stephan Alexander Würdtwein (Mainz, 1789), and one by Giles, *Sancti Bonifacii opera omnia*, Vol. I (London, 1844). All of these editions were based mainly upon manuscript 1.

The earliest edition of the modern historical school was that of Philipp Jaffé, *Sancti Bonifatii et Lulli epistolae*, in Volume III of his *Bibliotheca rerum Germanicarum, monumenta Moguntina* (Berlin, 1866). Jaffé used manuscripts 1 and 2 and attempted to standardize the chronology of the letters.

Twenty-six years later Ernst Dümmler published in the *Monumenta Germaniae historica*, in the section *Epistolae*, Vol. III: *S. Bonifatii et Lulli epistolae* (Berlin, 1892). Dümmler again re-

---

[1] *Vitae Bonifatii auctore Atloho libri duo*, in *Vitae sancti Bonifatii archiepiscopi Moguntini*, edited by Wilhelm Levison (Hanover, 1905).

vised the order of the letters. His conclusions have been modified somewhat by Michael Tangl, the most recent editor of the letters, but the latter, in order to facilitate cross reference from one edition of the *Monumenta* to the other, decided to keep the chronology of Dümmler in his own edition of 1916. Tangl's text is based primarily upon the Munich manuscript (Manuscript 1) carefully compared with Manuscripts 2 and 3.[1]

The present translation has been made from the text as published by Tangl. Some few letters there published have, however, been omitted from the translation, since they have no reference to the great bishop. For the sake of convenience in reference the letters as translated are numbered consecutively. The numbers appearing in brackets are those of the edition by Tangl.

Translations of the Bonifatian correspondence have appeared in several languages and with varying degrees of incompleteness. Worthy of mention are: Michael Tangl, *Die Briefe des heiligen Bonifatius*, 2d ed., in *Die Geschichtschreiber der deutschen Vorzeit*, Vol. XCII (Leipzig, 1912); Edward Kylie, *The English Correspondence of Saint Boniface* (London, 1924); G. W. Robinson, "Letters of Saint Boniface," a short selection in *Proceedings of the American Society of Church History* (2d ser., Vol. VII, p. 157).

Boniface's letters follow the usual fourfold pattern of greeting, preamble, main business, and conclusion. The form of greeting is only partially standardized, varying with the social or official status of the individual addressed. Expressions of affection are used in moderation; in fact, the writer's literary style is notably free from the extravagances in which some of his correspondents were apt to indulge.

The preamble states in general terms the motivation of the letter as a whole. It may take the form of an apology or a reference to former correspondence, sometimes giving in this way valuable hints in regard to obscure points of chronology, the sequence of events, or the relations of the persons concerned.

---

[1] In preparation for his edition Tangl published in the *Neues Archiv für ältere deutsche Geschichtskunde*, XL (1916), 639–790, and XLI (1917), 23–101, a complete report of his studies of the text.

The statement of the main business of the letter reflects most vividly the writer's personality. In general it follows the forms of courteous intercourse, but now and again it betrays currents of feeling which in a less well-controlled nature might easily have aroused antagonisms fatal to his main purpose. At such times it is interesting to note how greatly the style gains in force and clarity. Rhetorical decoration gives place to a simplicity which leaves no doubt as to the meaning. Even where the expression of individual opinion might seem dangerous, Boniface does not hesitate to say: "I think thus and so" or "as the case appears to me."

The conclusion generally sums up the contents of the letter and closes with good wishes for the welfare of the recipient in this world and the next.

LETTERS OF SAINT BONIFACE

Letters of Saint Boniface

I [9]. *Winfred to young Nithard, urging him to pursue his studies*
[716–717]

To his dearest companion and friend Nithard, to whom he has recently been drawn, not by the passing gift of gold nor the smoothness of flattering words, but by the affinity of spiritual sympathy and the bonds of unfailing love, Winfred sends greeting and wishes for eternal welfare in Christ Jesus.

From the utmost depths of my mediocrity I appeal to the splendid talents of your youth, my dearest brother, that you may not disregard the judgment of Solomon the wise: "In all thy works be mindful of thine end, and thou shalt be free from sin forever." And also: "Walk while ye have the light, lest darkness come upon you." For all things present shall swiftly pass away, but the things that shall abide forever are close at hand. All the precious things of this world such as gold and silver, or gems in glittering variety, or the luxury of dainty food, or elegant garments, if we fairly estimate them, pass away like shadow, vanish like smoke, disappear like foam, according to the unfailing opinion of the Psalmist: "As for man, his days are as grass; as a flower of the field, so he flourisheth." And again: "My days are like a shadow that declineth, and I am withered like grass." And hence all the wretched gold-pickers are described in Scripture as people condemned to keep nocturnal vigils, casting their nets like spiders' fragile webs, only to draw them in empty or catching but a little wind and dust. For, as the Psalmist says, they heap up riches and know not for whom they are doing it. And while the agent of the hated Pluto—that is to say, Death—gnashing his bloody teeth, barks at the door, they, all of a tremble and lacking all divine support, lose at once their precious souls and the deceitful treasure for which they had slaved like misers day and night. And then, snatched up by the hands of devils, they enter the most hideous caverns of Erebus to suffer there eternal punishment.

Now, all this being true beyond a doubt, I beg you earnestly and affectionately to give it your careful attention and hasten at once to revive the grace of natural talent which is born in you and not to extinguish the glowing spiritual flame of liberal learning and divine intelligence in the muddy water and sticky dust of earthly greed. Remember the words of the Psalmist speaking of the happy man: "His delight is in the law of the Lord, and in his law doth he meditate day and night." And again: "O, how love I thy law! It is my meditation all the day."[1] . . .

What, my dearest brother, is a more fitting pursuit for the young or a more valuable possession for the aged than a knowledge of Holy Scripture? Without peril of shipwreck from storm, it governs the vessel of the soul and leads it to the shore of a most charming paradise and the eternal joy of the angels above. . . .[2]

If it shall be God's will that I return to your country, as I purpose to do, I promise to be a faithful friend to you and in so far as my powers will allow, to be your devoted helper in your studies of Holy Scripture.

> Fare well, my brother, in youth's flower and strength,
> Mayst flourish with the Lord in His eternal home.
> Where martyrs hymn the King in heavenly choirs,
> And prophets and apostles add their meed of praise,
> Where, for eternity, the King of Kings His subjects dowers,
> There mayst thou bear the form of cherubin and seraphin,
> To the apostles heir, of prophets son,
> Nithard, avoid the dark contagion of this lowly earth,
> In punishment of Hell will it involve thee,
> The choirs above the heaven's blue seek to discover,
> Hosts singing to the God of Truth eternally
> Angelic canticles; there in the highest place,

[1] There follow quotations from Joshua 1:8, Job 28:17, 19, Proverbs 8:11, omitted in this translation.

[2] Quotations from Wisdom of Solomon 7:30–8:4 are here omitted.

Resplendent stand; the golden prize of Heaven's court
Draw down upon thy gleaming brows, and with thy praise
Hymn Christ on His celestial throne.[1]

II [10]. *Description of a vision seen by a monk of the monastery at Wenlock*[2] [716]

To the blessed virgin and best-loved lady, Eadburga, praise-worthy for her long perseverance in the observance of the monastic life, Winfred, one of the least in Christ Jesus, sends most affectionate greeting.

You have asked me, my dear sister, to describe to you in writing the marvelous visions of the man who recently died and came to life again in the convent of the Abbess Milburga, as they were revealed to him and were related to me by the venerable Abbess Hildelida. And now, thanks be to Almighty God, I am able to fulfill your wish more fully and more accurately because I myself spoke recently with the aforesaid resurrected brother when he returned to this country from beyond the seas. He then related to me in his own words the astounding visions which he saw in the spirit while he was out of the body.

He said that the extreme pain from a violent illness had suddenly freed his spirit from the burden of his body. He felt like a man seeing and wide-awake, whose eyes had been veiled by a dense covering and then suddenly the veil was lifted and everything made clear which had previously been invisible, veiled, and unknown. So with him, when the veil of the flesh was cast aside the whole universe seemed to be brought together before his eyes so that he saw in one view all parts of the earth and all seas and peoples. And angels of such pure splendor bore him up as he came forth from the body that he could not bear to gaze upon them.

[1] Translation by Edward Kylie, *The English Correspondence of Saint Boniface* (London, 1924), pp. 45–46. It is here reproduced with the kind permission of Chatto and Windus, the publishers.
[2] Compare No. XCII for an account of a similar vision.

With joyful and harmonious voices they sang: 'O Lord, rebuke me not in thy wrath; neither chasten me in thy hot displeasure.'

"They carried me up," he said, "high into the air, and I saw a mighty fire surrounding the whole earth, and flames of enormous size puffing up on high and embracing, as it were, in one ball the whole mechanism of the world, had not a holy angel checked it by the sign of the holy cross of Christ. For when the sign of the cross was made over against the threatening flame, it faded in great part and died away. I suffered intolerably from the heat, my eyes smarting and smitten by the glare of flashing spirits until an angel, splendid to look upon, laid his protecting hands upon my head and saved me from all injury by the flames."

He reported further that in the space of time while he was out of the body, a greater multitude of souls left their bodies and gathered in the place where he was than he had thought to form the whole race of mankind on earth. He said also that there was a crowd of evil spirits and a glorious choir of the higher angels. And he said that the wretched spirits and the holy angels had a violent dispute concerning the souls that had come forth from their bodies, the demons bringing charges against them and aggravating the burden of their sins, the angels lightening the burden and making excuses for them.

He heard all his own sins, which he had committed from his youth on and had failed to confess or had forgotten or had not recognized as sins, crying out against him, each in its own voice, and accusing him grievously. Each vice came forward as if in person, one saying: "I am your greed, by which you have most often desired things unlawful and contrary to the commands of God." Another said: "I am vainglory, by which you have boastfully put yourself forward among men." Another: "I am falsehood, whereby you have lied and sinned." Another: "I am the idle word you spoke in vain." Another: "I am sight, by which you have sinned by looking upon forbidden things." Another: "I am stubbornness and disobedience, whereby you have failed to obey your spiritual superiors." Another: "I am sluggishness and neglect in sacred studies." Another: "I am the wandering thoughts and useless notions in

which you have indulged too much both in church and elsewhere."
Another: "I am drowsiness, by which you were overcome so that
you were late to make your confession to God." Another: "I am the
idle errand." Another: "I am negligence and carelessness, which
have made you indifferent to the study of theology," and so forth.

Everything he had done in all the days of his life and had
neglected to confess and many which he had not known to be
sinful, all these were now shouted at him in terrifying words. In
the same way the evil spirits, chiming in with the vices, accusing
and bearing witness, naming the very times and places, brought
proofs of his evil deeds. He saw there, also, a certain man upon
whom he, while still numbered among the living, had inflicted a
wound and who, he said, was still living, but now was brought
in as a witness to his own misfortune. The bloody and open wound
and even the blood itself cried out against him, charging him with
the crime of bloodshed. And so, with his sins all piled up and
reckoned out, those ancient enemies declared him guilty and un-
questionably subject to their jurisdiction.

"On the other hand," he said, "the poor little virtues which I
had displayed unworthily and imperfectly spoke out in my defense." One said: 'I am obedience, which he has shown to his spiritual superiors.' And one: 'I am fasting, whereby he has chastened
his body against carnal desire.' Another: 'I am true prayer, which
he has uttered in the sight of God.' Another: 'I am the service
of the weak, which he has shown by kindness to the sick.' Another:
'I am the psalm, which he chanted before God to atone for an
idle word.' And so each virtue cried out for me in excuse for the
corresponding sin. And those angelic spirits in their boundless love
defended and supported me, while the virtues, greatly magnified
as they were, seemed to me far greater and more excellent than
could ever have been practiced by my own strength."

He reported further that he saw, as it were in the bowels of the
earth, many fiery pits vomiting forth terrible flames and, as the
foul flame arose, the souls of wretched men in the likeness of black
birds sat upon the margin of the pits clinging there for a while
wailing and howling and shrieking with human cries, mourning

their past deeds and their present suffering; then they fell scream-
ing back into the pits. And one of the angels said: "This brief
respite shows that Almighty God will give to these souls in the
judgment day relief from their punishment and rest eternal." But
beneath these pits in the lowest depths, as it were in a lower hell,
he heard a horrible, tremendous, and unspeakable groaning and
weeping of souls in distress. And the angel said to him: "The
murmuring and crying which you hear down there comes from
those souls to which the loving kindness of the Lord shall never
come, but an undying flame shall torture them forever."

He saw also a place of wondrous beauty, wherein a multitude
of very handsome men were enjoying extraordinary happiness, and
they invited him to come and share in their happiness if it were
permitted to him. And a fragrance of wonderful sweetness came
to him from the breath of the blessed souls rejoicing together.
The holy angels told him that this was the famed Paradise of God.

He saw also a pitch-black fiery river, boiling and glowing, dreadful and hideous to look upon. Over the river a log was placed
as a bridge. The holy and glorious souls, as they left their assembly,
hastened thither, anxious to cross to the other side. Some went
over steadily without faltering, but others, slipping from the log,
fell into the infernal stream. Some of these were plunged in nearly
over their heads, others only partly, some to the knees, some to
the waist, and some to the armpits. And yet, each one of those who
fell came up on the opposite bank far more brilliant and beautiful
than when he fell into the foaming and pitchy river. And one of
the blessed angels said of those fallen ones: "These are souls which
after this mortal life with some trifling sins not quite removed,
needed some kindly correction from a merciful God, that they
might be a worthy offering to him."

Beyond the river he beheld shining walls of gleaming splendor,
of amazing length and enormous height. And the holy angels
said: "This is that sacred and famous city, the heavenly Jerusalem,
where those holy souls shall live in joy forever." He said that those
souls and the walls of that glorious city to which they were hasten-

ing after they had crossed the river, were of such dazzling brilliance that his eyes were utterly unable to look upon them.

He related also that there came to this assembly the soul of a certain man who had died while holding the office of abbot, a soul which seemed to be of rare beauty. The evil spirits seized upon it, claiming it as belonging with them. But one of the angel choir replied: "I will quickly show you, miserable spirits, that this soul is certainly not in your power." Thereupon a great troop of purified souls broke in and said: "This was our elder and our teacher, and through his instruction he won us all to God; at that price he was redeemed, and clearly he is not in your power." So they joined with the angels in their fight against the demons, and with the help of the angels they snatched that soul away from the power of the evil spirits and set it free. Then an angel spoke in reproachful words, saying: "Now then, know ye and understand, ye wretched spirits, that you captured this soul unfairly, so away with you into everlasting fire!" Now, when the angel had spoken thus, the evil spirits broke into weeping and howling, and in a moment, as in the twinkling of an eye, they hurled themselves into the pits of glowing fire described above; after a brief interval, emerging again, they began anew their arguments about the merits of souls.

The man related also that it was vouchsafed to him to look upon the merits of divers men still living. Those who were free from blame and who, trusting to their holy virtues, were known to have the favor of God Almighty were ever safely guarded by angels with whom they were joined in intimate affection. But those who were befouled with dreadful crimes and the stains of a corrupt life were closely beset by a hostile spirit, who ever urged them on to evil deeds, and as often as they sinned in word or act, he held them up to the merriment of other infernal spirits. When a man sinned, the evil spirit never waited for him to sin again but straightway called each desperate offense to the notice of the other spirits. On the instant he persuaded the man to sin, he immediately reported the sin to the demons.

Among other stories, he told how he had seen a girl of this

world grinding grain. She saw lying near her a new distaff decorated with carving; she liked the looks of it and stole it. Then
five of the most horrible spirits, filled with huge delight, reported
the theft to their assembly and declared her guilty of theft. He
said also: "I saw the sad soul of a certain brother who had died
shortly before. I had ministered to him in his last sickness and had
performed his funeral services. On his deathbed he bade me go to
his brother, bear witness to his words, and, for the repose of his
soul, ask him to set free a certain bondwoman who had belonged
to them in common. But the brother, moved by avarice, did not
comply with his request. And so this soul, in deep distress, was
accusing his brother of breach of trust and was making loud complaints."

In the same way he bore witness concerning Ceolred, king of
Mercia, who, at the time these visions were seen, was unquestion-
ably still alive. He said that he saw the king protected by a certain
angelic screen against the assault of demons, as it were by a great
open book held above him.   But the demons begged the angels to
withdraw the protection and permit them to work their cruel wills
against him, charging him with a multitude of horrible crimes and
threatening to have him shut in the deepest dungeons of hell,
there to be racked with eternal torments as his sins deserved. Then
the angels, more sadly than was their wont, spoke: "Alas! that
this man of sin no longer permits himself to be protected, and
that we can give him no help on account of his own demerits."
So they withdrew the shelter of the protecting screen, and the
demons with triumphant rejoicings gathered together from every
part of the universe, in numbers greater than the narrator had
supposed there were human beings living in the world, and tormented the king with indescribable cruelties.

Then, finally, the blessed angels directed the man who had
seen and heard all these things in the spirit while he was set free
from his body, to return into his body at once. He was not to
hesitate to tell all that had been revealed to him to believers and
to those who should question him with a pious purpose, but should
refuse to talk to those who scoffed at him. He was to declare to a

certain woman dwelling far away all her sins one by one and was to explain to her how she might give satisfaction to Almighty God if she were so inclined. He should declare all his spiritual visions to a certain priest named Begga and afterward proclaim them before men according to Begga's instructions. His own sins, which had been charged against him by impure spirits, he was to confess and expiate according to the judgment of that priest and, as directed by an angelic precept, he should confide to the priest that he had already for many years, for the love of God and without the knowledge of any man, worn an iron girdle about his loins.

He declared that his own body, while he was out of it, was so offensive to him that in all his visions he saw nothing so hateful and so contemptible, nothing except the demons and the glowing fires, that exhaled such a foul stench as his own body. Even his brethren, whom he saw kindly performing his funeral rites, he hated because they took such care of that odious body. However, by the angels' command, at daybreak he entered again into his body just as he had left it at cockcrow. After his return he was unable for a whole week to see anything whatever with his bodily eyes, filled as they were with bleeding tumors [*fisicis*]. Later he proved by their own statements that what had been declared to him by the angels concerning the pious priest and the sinful woman was true. And shortly afterward the death of the wicked king proved that what he had seen of him was the truth.[1]

He reported also that he had seen many other similar visions which had slipped his memory, so that he could not recall the details, and he said that after those marvelous visions his memory was not as strong as it was before.

I have written down these things at your earnest request as he told them to me in the presence of three pious and most venerable brethren, who are known to be trustworthy witnesses and vouchers. Farewell, and may you live the life of angelic virginity, and reign forever with good report in heaven. Christ . . .[2]

[1] In a letter to King Ethelbald of Mercia, the successor of Coelred, who died in 716, Boniface again alludes to the evil life of the latter (see No. LVII).

[2] Beginning of an unfinished poem.

III [11]. *Bishop Daniel of Winchester gives Winfred a general letter of introduction* [718]

To all pious and merciful kings and princes, reverend and beloved bishops, holy abbots, priests and spiritual children sealed with the name of Christ, Daniel, servant of the servants of God, greeting.

While all commands of God are to be obeyed with sincere devotion, the witness of Holy Scripture proves how acceptable to Him is the hospitality shown to travelers. The blessed Abraham, on account of his kindly hospitality, was deemed worthy to receive holy angels in person and to enjoy their conversation. Lot also because of the same kindly service was snatched from the flames of Sodom. The grace of hospitality saved him from destruction by fire, because he obeyed the divine commands.

So may it profit your eternal welfare if you will extend to the bearer of these presents Winfred, a holy priest and servant of Almighty God, an affectionate welcome, such as God loves and prescribes. In receiving servants of God you receive Him whose majesty they also serve and Who promises: "He that receiveth you receiveth me." Doing this with heartfelt devotion, you will both fulfill the divine command and, trusting in the oracle of God, receive an everlasting reward in His presence.

May Supreme Grace keep Your Eminence safe from harm!

IV [12]. *Pope Gregory II entrusts the priest, Boniface, with the mission to the heathen* May 15, 719

Gregory, servant of the servants of God, to the devout priest Boniface.[1]

Your pious purpose, as it has been declared to us, and your well-proved sincerity of faith demand of us that we make use of you as our co-worker in spreading the divine words, which by the grace of God is our special care. Knowing, therefore, that you have been from childhood a student of sacred literature and that you now

[1] This is the first appearance of the name Boniface in place of Winfred.

wish, for the love of God, to extend the talent divinely entrusted to you, by dedicating yourself ceaselessly to missionary work and the teaching of the mystery of faith among the heathen, carrying to them the saving knowledge of the divine oracle, we rejoice in your loyalty and desire to further the work of grace vouchsafed to you. Wherefore, since with modest forethought you have laid before the Apostolic See your pious desire about the said mission, testing your design as a single member of a body submits itself to the sovereignty of the head, your humble submission to the direction of this head has placed your feet in the right path, and you have become as it were a perfectly articulated member of this body.

Therefore, in the name of the indivisible Trinity and by the unshaken authority of the blessed Peter, prince of the Apostles, whose government we administer by divine dispensation in his Holy See, we now place the modesty of your pious devotion upon a firm foundation and decree that with the word of God's grace, that flame of salvation which God came to earth to proclaim, you may go forth with His guidance to those peoples who are still in the bonds of infidelity. You are to teach them the service of the kingdom of God by the persuasion of the truth in the name of Christ, the Lord our God. You will pour into their untaught minds the preaching of both the Old and the New Testament in the spirit of virtue and love and sobriety and with reasoning suited to their understanding.

Finally, we enjoin upon you that, in admitting within the Church those who have already believed in God, you will insist upon using the sacramental discipline prescribed by the official ritual formulary of our Holy Apostolic See. Whatever you may find lacking in your work, you are to report to us as you have opportunity.

Fare you well.

Given on the Ides of May in the third year of our most pious and august lord, Leo, by God crowned emperor, in the third year of his consulship, in the second indiction.

To Winfred, holy father and true friend, worthy of honor, filled with the grace of piety and sacred learning Egburga, least of your disciples, whether men or women, wishes eternal welfare in the Lord.

As I acknowledge the bonds of your affection for me, my very inmost soul is filled with a sweetness as of honey. And though, for a while, having but just gained sight of you, I am deprived of your bodily presence, yet I ever clasp your neck in a sisterly embrace. And so, beloved, once my brother, you are now both father and brother in the Lord of Lords. For since cruel and bitter death has taken from me one whom I loved beyond all others, my own brother Oshere, I have cherished you in my affection above almost all other men. Not to waste further words: not a day nor a night goes by without some remembrance of your instruction.

Believe then, as God is my witness, that I hold you in deepest affection and trust that you are never unmindful of the friendship you surely had for my brother. Though I am far behind him in learning and far below him in character, yet in my regard for your affection I am his equal. Although the dark cloud of grief has grown lighter with the passage of time, it has never left me, rather the longer the time, the greater the sum of my sorrows, as it is written: "The love of man brings sorrow, but the love of Christ enlightens the heart." And when at the same time my dearest sister Wethburga vanished from my sight—a new wound and a new grief; she with whom I had grown up, whom I adored and who was nursed at the same mother's breast—Christ be my witness, everywhere was grief and terror and the dread of death. Gladly would I have died if it had so pleased God from whom no secrets are hid, or if slow-coming death had not deceived me.

But what shall I say now? It was not bitter death but a still more bitter and unexpected separation that divided us one from the other, leaving her, as I think, the happier and me the unhappy one to go on, like something cast aside, in my earthly service, while she, whom, as you know, I loved so tenderly, is reported to be

in a Roman cell as a recluse. But the love of Christ, which grew
and flourished in her breast, is stronger than all bonds, and "perfect love casteth out fear."

So I say: the lord of high Olympus wishes you happiness with
joy unspeakable because he has endowed you with sacred learning:
and in his law shalt thou meditate day and night. And it is
written: "How beautiful are the feet of them that bring glad tidings
of good things." She treads the hard and narrow way, while I lie
here below, bound by the law of the flesh as it were in shackles.
She, the happy one, shall declare in the day of judgment, as our
Lord did: "I was in prison and ye visited me." You, on the resur-
rection day, when the twelve Apostles shall sit upon their twelve
seats, shall sit there also, and as many as you shall have redeemed,
over so many shall you wear a crown of gold before the judgment
seat of the King Eternal. But I here in this vale of tears lament
my own sins as I deserve, because through them God has made me
unworthy to join with such companions.

Wherefore, believe me, more than the storm-tossed sailor longs
for the harbor, more than the thirsty fields desire rain, or the
anxious mother watches by the shore for her son, do I long for the
sight of you. But I am so oppressed by the tyranny of my sins and
weighed down by my countless faults that the hope of salvation
from impending danger cannot be mine, and I am plunged in
despair.

Wherefore, I, a sinner, cast myself at the feet of Your Eminence
and call to you out of the depths of my heart and from the ends
of the earth, O, my blessed master, to set me up upon the rock
of your prayers; for you are become my hope, my tower of
strength against my foes within and without. Comfort, I beseech
you, my unmeasured sorrow, quiet the waves of my grief, support
my weakness by your sustaining favor that it may not give way.

I beg you earnestly to send me some little remembrance, perhaps a holy relic or at least a few written words, that so I may
always have you with me.

Farewell, and may you prosper continually, making intercession
with God for me.

I too, Ealdbeoreth, a poor servant of Christ, salute you with all affection in the Lord. I beg you to remember in your inspired prayers the friendship you once promised me, and though we are separated in the body, may we be united in our memories.

VI [14]. *The abbess Eangyth and her daughter Heaburg [Bugga] to Boniface*   [719–722]

To the venerable Winfred, called Boniface, blessed of God in faith and love, endowed with the title of priest, crowned with the blossoms of chastity as with a garland of lilies, and learned in doctrine, Eangyth, unworthy handmaid of the handmaids of God and serving without merit under the name of abbess, also her only daughter Heaburg, called Bugga, send greeting in the Holy Trinity.

We have no words to express our thanks for the abundant affection you have shown to us in the letter brought by your messenger from beyond the sea. Well for us if your praise be truly sincere; but it is greatly to be feared that your undeserved praise may be rather reproof than laudation.

Beloved brother in spirit, not in the flesh, renowned for abundance of spiritual graces, to you alone have we desired to impart— and God is our only witness—by this tear-stained letter, under what a load of misery and what a crushing burden of worldly distractions we are weighed down. As when the whirlpools of the foaming sea draw in and out the mountainous waves dashing upon the rocks, when the force of the wind and the violence of the storm drive through a monstrous channel, the keels of ships are upturned and masts are shattered—even so the frail vessels of our souls are shaken by the mighty engines of our miseries and by the multitude of our misfortunes and, as the Word of Truth says of the house of the Gospel: "The rain descended and the floods came, and the winds blew, and beat upon that house," et cetera.

And first of all and above all, there are those external worldly affairs, which have kept us in turmoil, as I mentioned above, and the chain of innumerable sins, and the lack of full and perfect confidence that whatever we may do is good. We are worried, not only by the thought of our own souls, but—what is still more difficult and more important—by the thought of the souls of all who are entrusted to us, male and female, of diverse ages and dispositions, whom we have to serve and finally to render an account before the supreme judgment seat of Christ not only for our manifest failings, but also for those secret imaginings hidden from men and known to God alone. We have to carry on the fight with a single line of battle against a double one, with ten against twenty thousand. Then there is added the difficulty of our internal administration, the disputes over diverse sources of discord which the enemy of all good sows abroad, infecting the hearts of all men with bitter malice but especially monks and their orders, knowing, as he does, that "mighty men shall be mightily tormented."

We are further oppressed by poverty and lack of temporal goods, by the meagerness of the produce of our fields and the exactions of the king based upon the accusations of those who envy us; as a certain wise man says: "Witchcraft and envy darken many good things." So also our obligations to the king and queen, to the bishop, the prefect, the barons and counts. To enumerate all these would make a long story, much easier to imagine than to put into words.

To all these troubles must be added the loss of friends and compatriots, the crowd of relatives and the company of our kinsfolk. We have neither son nor brother, father nor uncle, only one daughter, whom death has robbed of all her dear ones, excepting one sister, a very aged mother, and a son of a brother, a man rendered unhappy because of his folly and also because our king has an especial grudge against his people. There is no other closely bound to us. God has taken them from us in various ways. Some have died in their native land, and their bodies rest in the foul dust of the earth to rise again in the day of judgment when the Lord's trumpet shall sound, and the whole race of men shall come forth from their dark tombs to render their account, and their spirits borne upon the arms of angels shall reign with Christ where sorrow

shall vanish, envy shall fade away, and pain and lamenting shall
flee before the face of the saints. But others have left their native
shores entrusting themselves to the pathways of the sea and have
sought the shrines of the Apostles Peter and Paul and of many
martyrs, virgins, and confessors whose names and number only
God knows.

For all these and similar reasons which could hardly be counted
in one day, even though, as the saying is, July and August should
lengthen out the hours of summer, our life is a weariness to us
and it is almost a burden to live. Everyone who is unequal to his
own task and distrusts his own judgment seeks a faithful friend
upon whose counsel he can rely and in whom he can have such
confidence that he will lay open to him every secret of his heart.
As is said: "What is sweeter than to have some one with whom
you can talk of everything as with yourself?" Therefore, on account of all those miseries which we have recounted at too great
length, we are compelled to seek a faithful friend, such a one in
whom we can confide better than in ourselves, who will consider
our pain and sorrow and want, will sympathize with us, console
and sustain us by his eloquence, and uplift us by his most wholesome discourse. Long have we sought, and now we believe that
we have found in you the friend whom we have wished, prayed,
and hoped for. And if God shall grant to us that through his angel
—as he sent the prophet Habbakuk into the lions' den with food
for Daniel the seer, and Philip, one of the seven deacons, to the
eunuch—we may be able to journey into those lands and upon
that pilgrimage in which you are engaged and, if we were permitted, to hear the living words from your lips: "How sweet are
thy words unto my taste! Yea, sweeter than honey to our mouth!"

But, since we have not been found worthy to do this, separated
as we are by a wide expanse of sea and land and the borders of
many states, still we desire you, Brother Boniface, to know, in that
confidence of which we made mention above, that we have long
wished to go to Rome, once mistress of the world, as many of our
friends, both relatives and strangers, have done. We would there
seek pardon for our sins as many others have done and are still

doing—especially I myself, more advanced in years and guilty of more offenses in my life. This desire of mine was known to the Abbess Wala formerly my spiritual mother and also to my only daughter, too young at that time to share my longing.

We are aware that there are many who disapprove of this ambition and disparage this form of devotion. They support their opinion by the argument that the canons of councils prescribe that everyone shall remain where he has been placed; and where he has taken his vows, there he shall fulfill them before God. But, since we all live by diverse impulses and the judgments of God are unknown and hidden from us—as the prophet says: "Thy righteousness is like the mountains of God and thy judgments are a great deep"—and since his secret will and pleasure in this matter are completely hidden from us, therefore, in these dark and uncertain problems, we beseech you with bowed heads to be our Aaron, that is, our mountain of strength, to support us by your prayers, to hold the censer of your intercessions as incense in the Divine Presence, and may the lifting up of your hands be like unto the evening sacrifice. We trust in God and beseech His mercy, that through the supplication of your mouth and your inmost prayers He may show us what He judges most profitable and useful: whether to live on in our native land or go forth upon our pilgrimage. We beg you also to be so kind as to send us word across the sea in reply to what we have scribbled in this letter in our rude, unpolished speech. We have little faith in those who "glory in appearance, but not in heart," but rather in your loyalty and your love toward God and your neighbor.

In regard to that before-mentioned brother, relative, and intimate friend of ours, named Denewald: if it should please God to direct his steps into those parts of the earth and that sojourn abroad in which you are engaged, we beg you to receive him with kindness and, if he shall so request, that you will send him on with your blessing and a favorable recommendation to the venerable brother, priest, and confessor Berhthere, who has long been occupied in that mission.

Farewell, brother in the spirit, most loyal, beloved with pure

and sincere affection, and may you be strong and prosper in our
beloved Lord. "A friend is long to seek, hard to find, and difficult
to keep." Pray for us that our many grievous sins may not work
against us.

VII [15]. *Bugga congratulates Boniface upon his success in Frisia*
[c. 720]

To Boniface or Winfred, venerable servant of God, endowed with
many symbols of spiritual gifts, most worthy priest of God, Bugga,
a humble housemaid, sends greetings of enduring affection.

Be it known to your gracious authority that I give thanks without ceasing to Almighty God, that, as I learn from the letter of
Your Holiness, He has shown His mercy to ·you in many ways,
leading you gently through lands unknown. First He inclined the
pontiff of the Glorious See to grant the desire of your heart. Next
He laid low before you Rathbod, that enemy of the Catholic
Church. Then he revealed to you in a dream that it was your duty
to reap the harvest of God, gathering in sheaves of holy souls
into the storehouse of the heavenly kingdom. Therefore I am the
more confident that no change of earthly conditions can turn me
away from the sheltering care of your affection. The power of love
grows warm within me, as I perceive that through the support
of your prayers I have reached the haven of a certain peace. And so
I humbly beg you again that you may be pleased to offer up to
God your earnest intercession for unworthy me, so that His grace
may keep me from harm through your protection.

Know also that the *Sufferings of the Martyrs* which you asked
me to send you I have not yet been able to get, but as soon as I can
I shall send it. And you, my best beloved, comfort my insignificance by sending me, as you promised in your dear letter, some
collection of the sacred writings.

I beg you further to offer some holy Masses for the soul of a
relative of mine who was dearest of all to me and whose name
was N . . .

I am sending you by this same messenger fifty *solidi* and an altar cloth, the best I can possibly do. Little as it is, it is sent with great affection.

Farewell in this world and "in love unfeigned."

VIII [16]. *The oath of Bishop Boniface*   Nov. 30, 722

In the name of the Lord God and of our Savior, Jesus Christ. In the sixth year of Leo, by the grace of God emperor, in the sixth year of his consulship and in the fourth year of his son, the Emperor Constantine, in the sixth indiction:

I, Boniface, by the grace of God bishop, promise to you, O blessed Peter, chief of the Apostles, and to your vicar, the blessed Pope Gregory and to his successors, in the name of the Father, the Son, and the Holy Spirit, the indivisible Trinity, and of this, thy most sacred body, that I will show entire faith and sincerity toward the holy catholic doctrine and will persist in the unity of the same, so God help me—that faith in which, beyond a doubt, the whole salvation of Christians consists. I will in no wise agree to anything which is opposed to the unity of the Church Universal, no matter who shall try to persuade me; but I will, as I have said, show in all things a perfect loyalty to you and to the welfare of your Church, to which the power to bind and loose is given by God, and to your vicar and his successors.

But, if I shall discover any bishops who are opponents of the ancient institutions of the holy Fathers, I will have no part nor lot with them, but so far as I can will restrain them or, if that is impossible, will make a true report to my apostolic master. But if (which God forbid!) I should be tempted into any action contrary to this my promise in any way or by any device or pretext whatsoever, may I be found guilty at the last judgment and suffer the punishment of Ananias and Sapphira, who dared to defraud you by making a false declaration of their property.

This text of my oath, I, Boniface, a humble bishop, have written with my own hand and laid above thy most sacred body. I have taken this oath, as is prescribed, in the presence of God, my witness and my judge, and I pledge myself to observe it.

IX [17]. *Pope Gregory II commends Bishop Boniface to all German Christians* · Dec. 1, 722

Gregory, bishop, servant of the servants of God, to all his reverend and holy brethren, fellow bishops, pious priests and deacons, glorious dukes, noble barons, counts, and all God-fearing Christians.

Hearing, to our great distress, that certain peoples in Germany on the eastern side of the Rhine are wandering in the shadow of death at the instigation of the ancient enemy and, as it were under the form of the Christian faith, are still in slavery to the worship of idols, while others who have not as yet any knowledge of God and have not been cleansed by the water of holy baptism but as pagans, to be likened unto the brutes, do not acknowledge their Creator, we have determined to send the bearer of these presents, our brother the reverend Bishop Boniface, into that country, for the enlightenment of both classes, to preach the word of the true faith, so that through his preaching of the word of salvation he may bring them eternal life. If perchance he shall find there some who have wandered from the way of the true faith or have fallen into error by the cunning persuasion of the devil, he is to correct them and bring them back into the haven of safety, teach them the doctrine of this Apostolic See and establish them firmly in that same catholic faith.

We exhort you, by your love of Christ and your reverence for his Apostles, to further all his efforts in every way and to receive him in the name of Jesus Christ, as it is written: "Whoso receiveth you receiveth me." We beg you to provide him with whatever is necessary, to furnish him with guides upon his way, to give him food and water or whatever he may require, so that by united effort and goodwill the work of benevolence entrusted to him and the mission of salvation may, with God's help, be promoted, that you may be worthy to win the reward of your labor and that merit for the conversion of the wanderers may be written to your account in Heaven. Whoever shall give aid and comfort to this servant of God, sent by this apostolic and catholic Church to enlighten the heathen, shall deserve the fellowship of the saints and martyrs of

Jesus Christ through the intercession of the leaders of the Apostles. But if (which God forbid!) anyone shall hinder his undertakings, or oppose the mission entrusted to him or his successors, by divine judgment he shall be smitten with the bonds of anathema and shall be subject to eternal damnation.

Given on the Kalends of December, in the seventh year of our most pious and august Lord Leo, by God crowned emperor, in the seventh year of his consulship and the fourth year of the Emperor Constantine his son, in the sixth indiction.

X [18]. *Pope Gregory II invests Boniface with episcopal authority*
Dec. 1, 722

Gregory, bishop and servant of the servants of God, to his best-beloved sons, both lay and clerical, living in Thuringia, greeting in the Lord.

We have made haste to comply with your praiseworthy desire by ordaining our brother and now fellow bishop Boniface as your prelate. We have laid our commands upon him that he shall never presume to confer unlawful ordinations, that he shall not admit to the sacred office one who has married a second time, or who has married a woman not a virgin, or who is illiterate, or is defective in any part of his body, or is under penance or a court order, or is known to be subject to any liability. If he shall find such persons already in office he shall not advance them. Africans who dare to apply for admission to ecclesiastical orders he may not accept upon any terms whatsoever; some of these are Manichaeans and others have often been shown to be rebaptized.[1]

The offices and adornment of the churches and whatever endowment they have he shall strive not to diminish but to increase. The revenue of the Church and the offerings of the faithful he is to divide into four parts: one for himself; one for the clergy according to the diligence with which they perform their duties; a third for the poor and for strangers; a fourth to be set aside for the

---

[1] On these Africans who were in Thuringia see Léon Godard, "Quels sont les Africains que le pape Grégoire II défendit en 723 d'élever au sacerdoce?" in *Revue Africaine* (1861), pp. 48–53.

maintenance of ecclesiastical buildings, and of these he is to render an account in the day of God's judgment. Ordinations of priests or deacons are not to take place except on the fast days of the fourth, seventh, and tenth months and also at the beginning of Lent and on the evening of the Saturday after Mid-Lent. The sacrament of baptism is to be administered only during Easter and Pentecost, except to those who are in peril of death lest they perish eternally.

As long as he shall observe the decrees of our see you are to obey him with devout hearts that the body of the Church may be at peace and without reproach through Christ our Lord who lives and reigns with God the Father Almighty and the Holy Spirit forever and ever.

May God preserve you from all evil, my best-beloved sons.

Given on the Kalends of December in the seventh year of our most pious and august Lord Leo, by God crowned emperor, in the seventh year of his consulship and in the fourth year of the Emperor Constantine his son, in the sixth indiction.

XI [19]. *Pope Gregory II commends Boniface to Thuringian leaders*   [Dec., 722]

Pope Gregory to his distinguished sons Asulf, Godolaus, Wilareus, Gundhareus, Alvoldus, and all faithful Thuringian Christians beloved of God.

The report of your glorious loyalty to Christ, how, when the heathen were pressing you to return to the worship of idols, you answered, full of confidence, that you would rather die than break the faith in Christ you had once accepted, was received by us with the greatest joy, and we returned thanks to our God and Redeemer, Giver of all good. We pray that, aided by His grace, you may advance to higher and greater things, clinging with all your might to your faith in the doctrine of the Holy Apostolic See. May you seek your reward, so far as the work of our holy religion requires, from this Holy Apostolic See, spiritual mother of all believers, as befits sons and joint heirs of a kingdom from a Royal Father.

We bid you also accept obediently in all ways the ministry of this our dearest brother Boniface, whom we have sent to you as a bishop consecrated to the office of preacher, well informed in the apostolic traditions, to be your instructor in the faith, and we urge you to coöperate with him for the perfection of your salvation in the Lord.

XII [20]. *Pope Gregory II recommends Boniface to Charles Martel*   [Dec., 722]

Pope Gregory to his son, the glorious duke Charles.

Knowing, best beloved in Christ, that you have shown a religious spirit upon many occasions, we notify Your Highness beloved of God that the bearer of these presents, our brother Boniface, a man of approved faith and character, consecrated bishop by us, well instructed in the traditions of the Holy Apostolic See over which we preside for the general welfare of the Church, has been sent by us to preach to the German peoples dwelling on the eastern side of the Rhine, fettered by pagan errors, many of them still lost in the darkness of ignorance.

For their sakes we warmly commend him to your high favor and pray you to help him in every need, to defend him against every enemy over whom you may prevail in the Lord's name, bearing in mind that whatever support you solicitously give to him will be given to God, who said that those who received his holy apostles, sent forth as a light to the Gentiles, would be receiving Himself. This prelate, instructed by us in the apostolic doctrine, goes forth to undertake this missionary work.

XIII [21]. *Pope Gregory III calls upon the Old Saxons to give up their heathen religion and to accept the teachings of Boniface*   [738–739]

Pope Gregory to all the people of the Province of Old Saxony.

Acknowledging my obligation toward the wise and the unwise, I desire you to know my anxious care in behalf of all of you, both those who have received the word of exhortation in the faith of our Lord Jesus Christ and those who are about to receive it, that your hearts may be comforted by instruction in love and in all the riches of abundant knowledge and in understanding of the mystery of God the Father and of Christ Jesus, as the great Apostle says: "In whom are hid all the treasures of wisdom and knowledge."

And this too I would say, since the Kingdom of God is at hand: Let no one henceforth deceive you with high-sounding words to seek salvation in the worship of idols made by hands, be they of gold or silver or brass or stone or any other substance. These lying deities, called gods by the heathen of old, are well known to be the dwelling places of demons. For all the gods of the Gentiles are demons, saith the Scripture, but the Lord our God is the creator of the heavens.

Those among you who have received our Lord Jesus Christ, let them walk in Him, rooted and grounded and confirmed in the faith, abounding in the works of grace. See to it that no one henceforth deceives you with the empty follies of philosophy. For the sons of darkness are more cunning than the children of light. Depart, my children, from the service of idols and come, worship the Lord our God "who made heaven and earth, the sea, and all that therein is," and you shall not be ashamed. For there is one God, of men and birds and beasts and fishes, blessed forever.

Put off, therefore, the old man and put on the new Christ, laying aside all anger, wrath, malice, blasphemy, and evil speaking; let them not come forth out of your mouth. Depart from the worship of idols, for the end of the day is near. Do not lie idle, but rather be active in good works, and Christ will dwell in you. And whatsoever you do, in word or in deed, do it in the name of our Lord Jesus Christ, giving thanks to God the Father through Him, casting off the way of the Gentiles, knowing that you have a Lord in the heavens. Lift up your hearts in fervent prayer to him: "For great is the Lord our God and greatly to be praised and terrible above all gods." It is His will that all men be saved and come to a knowledge of the truth.

This I enjoin upon you, my brethren, that whosoever among

you may desire to be converted to Christ, you shall in no way prevent him, neither compel him to worship graven images, for Christ the Lord lives with God the Father Almighty in the unity of the Holy Spirit forever and ever. Amen.

Beloved, our faithful fellow servant in the Lord, our brother and fellow bishop Boniface is sent to you that he may learn the conditions among you and may comfort your hearts with the word of exhortation in Christ Jesus our Lord, so that you may be delivered from the snares of the devil and be found worthy to be counted among the children of adoption and, set free from eternal damnation, may enter into everlasting life.

XIV [22]. *Charles Martel commends Boniface to all Frankish officials* [723]

To the holy and apostolic bishops, our fathers in Christ, and to the dukes, counts, vicars, palace officials, all our lower agents, our circuit judges [*missi*] and all who are our friends, the noble Charles, mayor of the palace, your well-wisher, sends greeting.

Be it known to you how that the apostolic man in Christ, Father Boniface, a man of apostolic character and a bishop, came to us with the request that we should take him under our guardianship and protection. Know that we have acquiesced with pleasure and, hence, have granted his petition before witnesses and commanded that this written order signed by our own hand be given him, that wheresoever he may choose to go, he is to be left in peace and protected as a man under our guardianship and protection to the end that he may render and receive justice. If he shall be in any need or distress which cannot be remedied according to law, let him and those dependent upon him come in peace and safety before our presence, so that no person may hinder or do him injury, but that he may rest at all times in peace and safety under our guardianship and protection.

And that this may the more surely be given credit, I have signed it with my own hand and sealed it with our ring.

XV [23]. *Bishop Daniel of Winchester advises Boniface on the method of conversion* [723–724]

To the venerable and beloved prelate Boniface, Daniel, servant of the people of God.

I rejoice, beloved brother and fellow priest, that you are deserving of the highest prize of virtue. You have approached the hitherto stony and barren hearts of the pagans, trusting in the plenitude of your faith, and have labored untiringly with the plowshare of Gospel preaching, striving by your daily toil to change them into fertile fields. To you may well be applied the Gospel saying: "The voice of one crying in the wilderness," etc. Yet a part of the second prize shall be given, not unfittingly, to those who support so pious and useful a work with what help they can give and supplement the poverty of those laborers with means sufficient to carry on zealously the work of preaching which has already been begun and to raise up new sons to Christ.

And so I have with affectionate good will taken pains to suggest to Your Prudence a few things that may show you how, according to my ideas, you may most readily overcome the resistance of those uncivilized people. Do not begin by arguing with them about the origin of their gods, false as those are, but let them affirm that some of them were begotten by others through the intercourse of male with female, so that you may at least prove that gods and goddesses born after the manner of men are men and not gods and, since they did not exist before, must have had a beginning.

Then, when they have been compelled to learn that their gods had a beginning since some were begotten by others, they must be asked in the same way whether they believe that the world had a beginning or was always in existence without beginning. If it had a beginning, who created it? Certainly they can find no place where begotten gods could dwell before the universe was made. I mean by "universe" not merely this visible earth and sky, but the whole vast extent of space, and this the heathen too can imagine in their thoughts. But if they argue that the world always existed without beginning, you should strive to refute this and to convince them by many documents and arguments. Ask your opponents who governed the world before the gods were born, who was the ruler? How could they bring under their dominion or subject to their law a universe that had always existed before them? And whence, or from whom or when, was the first god or goddess set up or begotten? Now, do they imagine that gods and goddesses still go on begetting others? Or, if they are no longer begetting, when or why did they cease from intercourse and births? And if they are still producing offspring, then the number of gods must already be infinite. Among so many and different gods, mortal men cannot know which is the most powerful, and one should be extremely careful not to offend that most powerful one.

Do they think the gods are to be worshiped for the sake of temporal and immediate good or for future eternal blessedness? If for temporal things, let them tell in what respect the heathen are better off than Christians. What gain do the heathen suppose accrues to their gods from their sacrifices, since the gods already possess everything? Or why do the gods leave it in the power of their subjects to say what kind of tribute shall be paid? If they are lacking in such things, why do they not themselves choose more valuable ones? If they have plenty, then there is no need to suppose that the gods can be pleased with such offerings of victims.

These and many similar things which it would take long to enumerate you ought to put before them, not offensively or so as to anger them, but calmly and with great moderation. At intervals you should compare their superstitions with our Christian doctrines, touching upon them from the flank, as it were, so that the pagans, thrown into confusion rather than angered, may be ashamed of their absurd ideas and may understand that their infamous ceremonies and fables are well known to us.

This point is also to be made: if the gods are all-powerful, beneficent, and just, they not only reward their worshipers but punish those who reject them. If, then, they do this in temporal matters, how is it that they spare us Christians who are turning almost the whole earth away from their worship and overthrowing their idols? And while these, that is, the Christians, possess lands rich in oil and wine and abounding in other resources, they have left to those, that is, the pagans, lands stiff with cold where their gods, driven out of the world, are falsely supposed to rule. They are also frequently to be reminded of the supremacy of the Christian world, in comparison with which they themselves, very few in number, are still involved in their ancient errors.

If they boast that the rule of the gods over those peoples has been, as it were, lawful from the beginning, show them that the whole world was once given over to idol-worship, until by the grace of Christ and through the knowledge of one God, its Almighty Founder and Ruler, it was enlightened, brought to life, and reconciled to God. For what is the daily baptism of the children of believing Christians but purification of each one from the uncleanness and guilt in which the whole world was once involved?

I have been glad to call these matters to your attention, my brother, out of my affection for you, though I suffer from bodily infirmities so that I may well say with the Psalmist: "I know, O Lord, that thy judgments are right and that thou in faithfulness hast afflicted me." Wherefore I earnestly pray Your Reverence and all those who serve Christ in spirit to make supplication for me that the Lord Who gave me to drink of the wine of remorse, may be swift in mercy, that He who was just in condemnation may graciously pardon, and by His mercy enable me to sing in gratitude the words of the Prophet: "In the multitude of my thoughts within me thy comforts delight my soul."

I pray for your welfare in Christ, my very dear colleague, and beg you to bear me in mind.

XVI [24]. *Reply of Pope Gregory II to a report of Boniface*
Dec. 4, 724

Gregory, servant of the servants of God, to the most reverend and most holy brother Boniface, his fellow bishop, greeting.

Moved by zeal for the task entrusted to us, as well as by the Gospel precept, "Pray ye, therefore, the Lord of the harvest that he send forth laborers into his harvest," we directed you, reverend brother, in imitation of the Apostles ordered by the Lord: "Go forth and preach the Gospel!" . . . "Freely ye have received; freely give," into the lands of the West, for the enlightenment of the people of Germany sitting in the shadow of death, expecting you to reap profit therefrom, for the future, like that faithful servant in the Scripture in dealing with his talent. We have perceived the fragrance of the ministry of the Word arising from your gift of obedience and we have learned that through the broadcasting of your preaching, as you have reported, the unbelieving people are being converted. Wherefore we give thanks to the power of the Lord and pray that He, from whom all good proceeds and whose will it is that all men shall come to a knowledge of the truth, may work with you and may lead that people out of darkness into light by the inspiration of His might. We believe that hence a bountiful reward shall be written down for you in heaven. If you persevere you will be able to say with the Apostle: "I have fought a good fight, I have finished my course, I have kept the faith."

But, to win the crown of your labor, keep on! For God promises salvation to those who shall endure unto the end. Let no threats alarm you, no fears cast you down, but holding fast to your faith in God, proclaim the word of truth. The completion shall come by divine aid, as long as the will to do the good work persists. How many you have turned from their errors we have learned from your written report, which we have carefully examined, and we give our deepest gratitude to God, rejoicing in this harvest of souls.

As for that bishop[1] who up to the present time has failed, through a certain slothfulness, to spread through the same region the word of preaching but now claims for himself a part therein as belonging within his jurisdiction, we have written a fatherly letter to our most excellent son, Charles the Patrician, urging him to keep the former in check, and we believe that he will give orders to prevent this wrong.

But do you cease not to preach the word of salvation "in season and out of season."

[1] Gerold of Mainz.

Finally, we have not failed to write to the Thuringians and to the people of Germany all that pertains to the welfare and salvation of souls. Among other things we have enjoined upon them to organize bishoprics and to found churches. For He who desires not the death of a sinner, but rather that he turn from his wickedness and live, will in all things give the increase.

May God keep you in safety.

Given on the second day before the Nones of December, in the eighth year of our most pious and august Lord Leo, by God crowned emperor, in the eighth year of his consulship and the fifth year of the Emperor Constantine, his son, in the eighth indiction.

XVII [25]. *Pope Gregory II commends Boniface to the Thuringians*   [Dec., 724]

Gregory, servant of the servants of God, to all the people of the Thuringians.

The Lord Jesus Christ, Son of God and very God, descended from Heaven, was made man, deigned to suffer and be crucified for us, was buried, rose from the dead on the third day, and ascended into Heaven. To His holy Apostles and disciples He said: "Go forth and teach all peoples, baptizing them in the name of the Father, the Son, and the Holy Spirit"; and He promised those who believed in Him eternal life.

We, therefore, desiring that you may rejoice with us forever where there is no ending, neither sorrow nor any bitterness, but eternal glory, have sent to you our most holy brother, Bishop Boniface, that he may baptize you and teach you the doctrine of Christ and lead you out of error into the way of safety, that you may win salvation and life eternal. But do you be obedient unto him in all things, honor him as your father, and incline your hearts to his instruction, for we have sent him to you, not for any temporal gain, but for the profit of your souls. Therefore love God and receive baptism in his name, for the Lord our God has prepared for those who love him things which the eye of man hath not seen, and which have never entered into the heart of man.

Depart from evil doing, and do what is right. Worship not idols, neither sacrifice offerings of flesh to them, for God does not accept such things, but observe and do as our brother Boniface shall direct, and you and your children shall be in safety forever.

Build also a house where this your father and bishop may live and churches where you may offer up your prayers, that God may forgive your sins and grant you eternal life.

XVIII [26]. *Replies of Pope Gregory II to questions of Boniface*
Nov. 22, 726

Gregory, servant of the servants of God, to his most reverend and holy brother and fellow bishop Boniface.

Your messenger, the pious priest Denuald, has brought us the welcome news that you are well and prospering, with the help of God, in the service for which you were sent. He also brought a letter from you showing that the field of the Lord which had been lying fallow, bristling with the thorns of unbelief, has received the plowshare of your instruction, plowing in the seed of the word, and is bringing forth an abundant harvest of true belief.

In this same letter you inserted several paragraphs of inquiries as to the faith and teaching of this Holy and Apostolic Roman Church. And this was well done; for the blessed apostle Peter stands as the fountainhead of the apostolate and the episcopate. And to you who consult us about ecclesiastical matters we show what decision you have to take according to the teaching of apostolic tradition, and we do this not as if by our own personal authority, but by the grace of Him who opens the mouth of the dumb and makes eloquent the tongues of infants.

You ask first within what degrees of relationship marriage may take place. We reply: strictly speaking, in so far as the parties know themselves to be related they ought not to be joined together. But since moderation is better than strictness of discipline, especially toward so uncivilized a people, they may contract marriage after the fourth degree.

As to your question, what a man is to do if his wife is unable,

on account of disease, to fulfil her wifely duty: it would be well if
he could remain in a state of continence. But, since this is a matter
of great difficulty, it is better for him who cannot refrain to take
a wife. He may not, however, withdraw his support from the one
who was prevented by disease, provided she be not involved in
any grievous fault.

In regard to a priest or any cleric accused by the people: unless the evidence of the witnesses to the charge against him is
positive, let him take oath before the assembly, calling as witness
of his innocence Him to whom all things are plain and open; and
so let him keep his proper standing.

In the case of one confirmed by a bishop, a repetition of this rite
is prohibited.

In the celebration of the Mass, the form is to be observed which
our Lord Jesus Christ used with his disciples. He took the cup
and gave it to them, saying: "This cup is the new testament in my
blood; this do ye as oft as ye take it." Wherefore it is not fitting
that two or three cups should be placed on the altar when the
ceremony of the Mass is performed.

As to sacrificial foods: You ask whether, if a believer makes the
life-giving sign of the cross above them, it is permitted to eat them
or not. A sufficient answer is given in the words of the blessed
apostle Paul: "If any man say unto you, This is offered in sacrifice
unto idols, eat not for his sake that shewed it, and for conscience
sake."

You ask further, if a father or mother shall have placed a young
son or daughter in a cloister under the discipline of a rule, whether
it is lawful for the child after reaching the years of discretion to
leave the cloister and enter into marriage. This we absolutely forbid, since it is an impious thing that the restraints of desire should
be relaxed for children offered to God by their parents.

You mention also that some have been baptized by adulterous
and unworthy priests without being questioned whether they believe, as it is in the ritual. In such cases you are to follow the
ancient custom of the Church. He who has been baptized in the
name of the Father, Son, and Holy Spirit may on no account be
baptized again; for he has received the gift of His grace not in

the name of the one who baptizes, but in the name of the Trinity. Let the word of the Apostle be observed: "One God, one faith, one baptism." We require you to convey spiritual instruction to such persons with especial zeal.

As to young children taken from their parents and not knowing whether they have been baptized or not, reason requires you to baptize them, unless there be someone who can give evidence in the case.

Lepers, if they are believing Christians, may receive the body and blood of the Lord, but they may not take food together with persons in health.

You ask whether, in the case of a contagious disease or plague in a church or monastery, those who are not yet attacked may escape danger by flight. We declare this to be the height of folly; for no one can escape from the hand of God.

Finally, your letter states that certain priests and bishops are so involved in vices of many sorts that their lives are a blot upon the priesthood and you ask whether it is lawful for you to eat with or to speak with them, supposing them not to be heretics. We answer, that you by apostolic authority are to admonish and persuade them and so bring them back to the purity of church discipline. If they obey, you will save their souls and win reward for yourself. You are not to avoid conversation or eating at the same table with them. It often happens that those who are slow in coming to a perception of the truth under strict discipline may be led into the paths of righteousness by the influence of their table companions and by gentle admonition. You ought also to follow this same rule in dealing with those chieftains who are helpful to you.

This, my dear brother, is all that need be said with the authority of the Apostolic See. For the rest we implore the mercy of God, that He who has sent you into that region in our stead and with apostolic authority and has caused the light of truth to shine into that dark forest by means of your words may mercifully grant the increase, so that you may reap the reward of your labors and we may find remission for our sins.

God keep you in safety, most reverend brother.

Given on the tenth day before the Kalends of December, in the tenth year of our most pious and august Lord Leo, by God crowned emperor, in the tenth year of his consulship and the seventh of the Emperor Constantine his son, in the tenth indiction.

XIX [27]. *Boniface gives advice to Abbess Bugga regarding her pilgrimage to Rome* [Before 738]

To the beloved lady, Abbess Bugga, sister and dearest of all women in Christ, Boniface, a humble and unworthy bishop, wishes eternal salvation in Christ.

I desire you to know, dearest sister, that in the matter about which you wrote asking advice of me, unworthy though I am, I dare neither forbid your pilgrimage on my own responsibility nor rashly persuade you to it. I will only say how the matter appears to me. If, for the sake of rest and divine contemplation, you have laid aside the care for the servants and maids of God and for the monastic life which you once had, how could you now subject yourself with labor and wearing anxiety to the words and wishes of men of this world? It would seem to me better, if you can in no wise have freedom and a quiet mind at home on account of worldly men, that you should obtain freedom of contemplation by means of a pilgrimage, if you so desire and are able, as our sister Wiethburga did. She has written me that she has found at the shrine of St. Peter the kind of quiet life which she had long sought in vain. With regard to your wishes, she sent me word, since I had written to her about you, that you would do better to wait until the rebellious assaults and threats of the Saracens who have recently appeared about Rome should have subsided. God willing, she will then send you an invitation. To me also this seems the best plan. Make ready what you will need for the journey, wait for word from her, and then act as God's grace shall command.

In regard to the writings which you have requested of me, you must excuse my remissness, for I have been prevented by pressure of work and by my continual travels from completing the book you ask for. When I have finished it, I shall see that it is sent to you.

In return for the gifts and garments you have sent me, I offer my grateful prayers to God that he may give you a reward with the angels and the archangels in the highest heavens. I exhort you, then, in God's name, my very dear sister—nay mother and most sweet lady—to pray earnestly for me, since for my sins I am wearied with many sorrows and am far more disturbed by anxiety of mind than by the labor of my body. May you rest assured that the long-tried friendship between us shall never be found wanting.

Farewell in Christ.

XX [28]. *Pope Gregory III promotes Boniface to the rank of missionary archbishop and sends him the pallium* [c. 732]

To our very reverend and holy brother and fellow bishop, Boniface, sent by this Apostolic Church of God to enlighten the people of Germany and those in the surrounding countries who are still lingering in the shadow of death and involved in error, Gregory, servant of the servants of God, sends greeting.

It was with great satisfaction that we learned from a repeated reading of the letter from Your Sacred Fraternity that by the grace of Jesus Christ multitudes have been converted by you from paganism and error to a knowledge of the true faith. We, together with the whole Church, applaud such an increase, as we are taught in the parable of him to whom five talents were given and who gained also other five. For this we have ordered the gift of a sacred pallium to be sent to you to be received and worn by the authority of the Holy Apostle Peter, and we direct you to be recognized as an archbishop by divine appointment. How you are to use it you will learn by apostolic instructions; namely, you are to wear it solely when you are celebrating a solemn mass or when you may have occasion to consecrate a bishop.

But, since you declare yourself unable to impart the means of salvation to all who are converted to the true faith in those parts, since the faith has already been carried far and wide, we command you, in accordance with the sacred canons and by authority of the

Apostolic See to ordain bishops wherever the multitude of the faithful has become very great. Do this, however, after prayerful reflection, lest the dignity of the episcopate be impaired.

As to that priest who, you say, came to us a year ago and received from us absolution for his crimes, be advised that he made no confession to us, nor did he receive from us any absolution that he might return to his evil lusts. If you find him given over to error, we order you, by the power of the Apostolic See, to discipline him according to the sacred canons, him and any others like him, if perchance you find such. When he came hither he said, "I am a priest," and he asked us for a letter of recommendation to our son Charles [Martel], and that was the only favor we granted him. If he conducts himself badly, we desire you to put him under a ban, him and all the rest of them.

Those who, you say, were baptized by pagans we order you to baptize again in the name of the Trinity, if the fact is proved.

You say, among other things, that some have the habit of eating wild horses and very many eat tame horses. This, holy brother, you are in no wise to permit in future but are to suppress it in every possible way, with the help of Christ, and impose suitable penance upon the offenders. It is a filthy and abominable practice.

You inquire whether offerings for the dead are permitted. The teaching of Holy Church is that anyone may make offerings for his truly Christian dead, and that the priest may remember them in his prayers. And, although we are all subject to sin, it is fitting for the priest to remember the faithful dead and he should make intercession for them; not, however, for the ungodly, even if they were Christians, shall such service be allowed.

We direct that those who are uncertain whether they have been baptized or not and those who were baptized by a priest who also sacrificed to Jupiter and who ate of sacrificial food are to be baptized [again].

We decree, that [in contracting marriage] every one shall observe the rules of relationship even to the seventh degree.

In so far as you are able, prevent a man who has lost his wife from marrying again in the future more than once.

One who has murdered his father, mother, brother, or sister may not receive the body of the Lord so long as he shall live, excepting at the moment of death as a *viaticum*. Let him also abstain from eating flesh or drinking wine during his natural life. Let him fast on the second, fourth, and sixth day of the week, and thus with lamentation wash away the offense he has committed.

You say that among other evil practices in those parts, some Christians are in the habit of selling slaves to the heathen for sacrifice. This, my brother, you are especially to forbid and prevent in the future. It is an impious crime, and you are to impose upon the guilty person penance similar to that for homicide.

Whenever you ordain a bishop let two or three other bishops be with you, that your action may be acceptable to God and that you may perform the consecration with their approval and in their presence.

These things, beloved brother, we desire you diligently to observe. Carry on with earnest devotion the work of salvation already begun, so that you may receive for the riches that you have contributed a reward of eternal blessedness from the Lord our God.

We have had made out the privilege you request. We send it with this letter, praying that you may receive the fullest and most complete reward under the protection of the Lord our God, for the conversion of the erring to Christ our God.

May God preserve you in safety, most reverend brother.

XXI [29]. *The English nun Lioba asks the prayers of Boniface for her parents*   [Soon after 732]

To my revered master Boniface, bearing the insignia of the highest office, most dear to me in Christ and bound to me by ties of kinship, I, Lioba, least of the servants of those who bear the easy yoke of Christ, wish enduring health and prosperity.

I beg you graciously to bear in mind your ancient friendship for my father, Dynne, formed long ago in the West country. It is now eight years since he was called away from this world, and I ask your prayers for his soul. I recall to your memory also my

mother, Aebbe, who, as you know, is bound to you by ties of
blood. She lives a life of suffering, bowed down by grievous illness.
I am the only daughter of my parents and, unworthy though I be,
I wish that I might regard you as a brother; for there is no other
man in my kinship in whom I have such confidence as in you.
I have ventured to send you this little gift, not as if it deserved
even a kindly glance from you but that you may have a reminder
of my insignificance and not let me be forgotten on account of our
wide separation. May the bond of our true affection be knit ever
more closely for all time. I eagerly pray, my dear brother, that
I may be protected by the shield of your prayers from the poisoned
darts of the hidden enemy. I beg you also to be so kind as to correct the unskilled style of this letter and to send me, by way of
example, a few kind words which I greatly long to hear.

I have composed the following verses according to the rules of
poetic art, not trusting to my own presumption, but trying only
to exercise my little talents and needing your assistance. I have
studied this art under the guidance of Eadburga, who still carries
on without ceasing her investigation of the divine law.

Farewell, and may you live long and happily, making intercession for me.

> The omnipotent Ruler who alone created everything,
> He who shines in splendor forever in His Father's kingdom,
> The perpetual fire by which the glory of Christ reigns,
> May preserve you forever in perennial right.[1]

XXII [30]. *Boniface thanks the abbess Eadburga for a gift of
books*   [735-736]

To his beloved sister, the abbess Eadburga, to whom he has long
since been bound by the ties of spiritual propinquity, Boniface,
servant of the servants of God, wishes eternal welfare in Christ.

May He who rewards all righteous acts cause my dearest sister
to rejoice in the choir of angels above because she has consoled

---

[1] These awkward verses, written by a beginning student of poetry, contain an
invocation of the Trinity—the Father who created, the Son who shines in his
Father's kingdom, and the Spirit *iugiter flagrans*.

with spiritual light by the gift of sacred books an exile in Germany who has to enlighten the dark corners of the Germanic peoples and would fall into deadly snares if he had not the Word of God as a lamp unto his feet and a light upon his path.

Trusting in your affection, I earnestly beg you to pray for me because, for my sins, I am tossed by the tempests of a perilous sea. Pray to Him who dwells on high but looks after the lowly, that He may forgive my faults and lend me His word in the opening of my mouth, so that the gospel of the glory of Christ may run its course and be made manifest among the nations.

XXIII [32]. *Boniface to Bishop Pehthelm of Whithorn in Scotland on the marriage of a godfather with the mother of a child*

[735]

To his reverend brother and beloved fellow bishop, Pehthelm, Boniface, humble servant of the servants of God, sends sincere greetings of love in Christ.

We turn to the fatherly kindness of Your Holiness with earnest supplication, because we feel ourselves in serious peril, and beg you to aid us with your prayers acceptable to God. This German ocean is dangerous for sailors and we pray that we may reach the haven of eternal peace without stain or injury to our soul, and that while we are striving to offer the light of Gospel truth to the blind and ignorant who are unwilling to gaze upon it, we may not be wrapped in the darkness of our own sins, neither "run or have run in vain," but, upheld by your intercessions, may we go forward unspotted and enlightened into the splendor of eternity.

We are sending you some little gifts: a garment decorated with white spots and a coarse towel to dry the feet of the servants of God. Deign to accept them, we beg you, as a reminder of us.

There is one matter about which we desire your opinion and your advice. The priests throughout Gaul and Frankland maintain that for them a man who takes to wife a widow, to whose child he has acted as godfather, is guilty of a very serious crime. As to the nature of this sin, if it is a sin, I was entirely ignorant, nor have I ever seen it mentioned by the fathers, in the ancient canons, nor in the decrees of popes, nor by the Apostles in their catalogue of sins. If you have found anywhere a discussion of this subject in ecclesiastical writings kindly inform us and let us know also your own opinion.

I desire, for Christ's sake, that Your Welfare may advance in all holy virtues, with health and long life.

XXIV [33]. *Boniface asks Archbishop Nothelm of Canterbury to forward a copy of the questions sent to Pope Gregory I by the Anglo-Saxon missionary, Augustine, and the Pope's answers thereto*   [735]

To his beloved master, Archbishop Nothelm, clothed with the insignia of the highest pontificate, Boniface, a humble servant of the servants of God, sends sincere greeting of eternal love in Christ.

I earnestly beseech your gracious favor, that you may be pleased to remember me in your holy prayers, and thus the vessel of my mind, tossed by the recurrent storms of the various Germanic tribes, may by your prayers be brought into a safe and rock-bound harbor. May I be united with you in a brotherly communion no less firm than was granted me by your predecessor, Archbishop Bertwald of reverend memory, at the time I left the country. May I and also my brethren and companions in my journeys be worthy to be united with you in the bond of the spirit, in the ties of love, in the unity of my catholic faith and in the sweetness of spiritual affection.

I beg also that you will procure for me a copy of the letter containing, it is said, the questions of Augustine, first prelate and preacher of the English, and the replies of the sainted Pope Gregory [I]. In this writing it is stated, among other things, that marriages between Christians related in the third degree are lawful. Now will you cause an inquiry to be made with the most scrupulous care whether or not that document has been proved to be by the aforenamed father, Saint Gregory. For the registrars [*scriniarii*] say that it is not to be found in the archives of the Roman church among the other documents of the aforesaid pope.

Further, I desire your counsel in regard to a sin which I have unwittingly committed by granting to a certain man the right to marry. It happened in this way: the man, like many others, had stood as godfather to the child of another and then after the death of the father had married the mother. The Romans declare that this is a sin, even a capital sin, and say that in such cases a divorce should take place. They say that under Christian emperors, such a marriage was punishable by death or by perpetual exile. If you find that this is accounted so great a sin in the decrees of catholic fathers or in the canons or even in Holy Writ, pray let me know it, so that I may understand and know what is the authority for such an opinion. I cannot possibly understand how, on the one hand, spiritual relationship in the case of matrimonial intercourse can be so great a sin, while, on the other hand, it is well established that by holy baptism we all become sons and daughters, brothers and sisters of Christ and the Church.

I beg also that you will let me know in what year of the Incarnation of Christ the first missionaries sent by Saint Gregory to the English people arrived.

Farewell.

XXV [34]. *Boniface asks his former pupil, Abbot Duddo, to send him certain manuscripts* [735]

To his beloved son, Abbot Duddo,[1] Boniface, called also Winfred, servant of the servants of God, sends a heartfelt greeting of love in Christ.

I hope, my dear son, that you remember the saying of a certain wise man—"Keep thy old friend"—and forget not in old age the ancient friendship which we began in our youth and have preserved till now, but remember your father, now failing in strength and approaching in every limb the way of all earthly things. Though I was but poorly equipped as a teacher, I have striven to be the

---

[1] The identity of this Duddo is doubtful. It is possible but not probable that he was in some way connected with the papal archives in Rome.

most devoted to you of them all, as you yourself bear witness. Be mindful of this devotion and take pity upon an old man, worn out by the storms of the German sea. Try to support me by pouring out your prayers to God and help me with the Sacred Writings and the inspired treatises of the Holy Fathers. Since a spiritual tract is well known to be a teacher for those who read the Holy Scriptures, I beg you to procure for me, as an aid in sacred learning, a part of a treatise upon the Apostle Paul, which I lack. I have tracts upon two epistles, one upon Romans, the other upon First Corinthians. Further, whatever you may find in your church library which you think would be useful to me and which I may not be aware of or may not have in written form, pray let me know about it, as a loving son might do for an ignorant father, and send me also any notes of your own.

And, if you please, let us mutually agree to render such service to each other. In accord with what my son, the priest Eoban, who brings my letters, may say to you about the marriage of a woman to the godfather of her children, kindly search the records to find out by what authority this is held to be a capital crime among the Romans. If you find in ecclesiastical writings any discussion of this sin, please inform me of it at once.

We wish you health and prosperity in Christ.

XXVI [35]. *Boniface asks the abbess Eadburga to make him a copy of the Epistles of St. Peter in letters of gold*　　　[735]

To his most reverend and beloved sister, the abbess Eadburga, Boniface, humble servant of the servants of God, sends heartfelt greetings of love in Christ.

I pray to Almighty God, the rewarder of all good works, that He will repay you in the heavenly mansions and eternal tabernacles and in the choir of the blessed angels for all the kindnesses you have shown me, the solace of books and the comfort of the garments with which you have relieved my distress.

And I beg you further to add to what you have done already

by making a copy written in gold of the Epistles of my master, St. Peter the Apostle, to impress honor and reverence for the Sacred Scriptures visibly upon the carnally minded to whom I preach. I desire to have ever present before me the words of him who is my guide upon this road. I am sending by the priest Eoban the materials for your writing.

Do then, dearest sister, with this petition of mine as you have always done with my requests, so that here also your works may shine forth in golden letters for the glory of our heavenly Father. I pray for your well-being in Christ, and may you go on upward to still greater heights of holy virtue.

XXVII [36]. *Sigebald, a priest, renews his request that he might consider Boniface his bishop in conjunction with his regular diocesan, Daniel of Winchester* [732–745]

To the most reverend prelate, known for his fatherly kindness, Archbishop Boniface, Sigebald, unworthy and humble servant of the servants of God, sends hearty greetings in the Lord.

With humble prayer, bowing before you, as it were, upon bended knees, I beg you to grant the request which I sent to you by your priest Eoban, asking him to let you know my wish to have you for my bishop as well as my own bishop, Daniel. I am sure that if he had done his part as I requested, you would have granted my petition out of kindness to me, and I had expected to receive from you, my lord, a consoling letter.

I wish you to know that, from that time on, I have added your name to those of our bishops whenever I have celebrated Mass, and I shall continue to do so as long as I live. If I survive you I shall add your name to that of our father, Bishop Ernwald. I wish to mention that in writing to you about this I do not rely upon any merit of my own, sinner that I am, but upon the mercy of God and the hope you have in Him.

So I pray you to remember me both now and in the future so far as my insignificance may deserve.

Farewell in Christ.

XXVIII [37]. *An unnamed person (perhaps Lullus) sends a letter of condolence to one Si(gebald)*   [735–786]

To the most reverend brother and veteran of Christ, SI, greetings of divine welfare in God on high.

I have learned from certain venerable servants of God that you are suffering from a severe attack of illness and are in great pain and much exhausted, though not greatly disheartened. When I heard this I gave thanks to God that you had been visited with heavenly grace, enriched with divine gifts, and favored with spiritual tokens. This visitation from a chastening God is a call to you to join yourself to Him with eager desire and a love that never fails. So let this word never escape your memory: "The king hath desired thy beauty." Upon careful reflection you will be aware that, although for the moment you are afflicted by the hand of a chastening and loving God, you are being prepared for your soul's eternal welfare; for God "scourgeth every son whom he receiveth." You may say with joyful satisfaction in the words of the Apostle Paul: "When I am weak, then am I strong," and, "My strength is made perfect in weakness." Frailty of the body is strength of the spirit, and so you shall be found worthy to be a son of the Most High, who bids you to the chamber of the Eternal King.

I pray for your speedy recovery and your well-being in Christ.

XXIX [38]. *Boniface requests the prayers of Abbot Aldherius for himself and for the German idolaters*   [732–754]

To his reverend brother, Abbot Aldherius, Boniface, humble servant of the servants of God, sends greeting in Christ.

From the depths of my heart I beg your gracious love to bear me in mind in your holy prayers and I urge you to implore for me our merciful God, who is the author of our wanderings, that He will hold our frail vessel in His guiding and protecting hand, preserve it from the waves of the German tempests, and bring it safely to the peaceful shore of the heavenly Jerusalem. Salute all our dear brethren in God in your holy community with our kiss of love and devotion. We commend ourselves to your prayers, so that, living or dying, we may be one with you in loving communion. And to make stronger this bond between us, we shall strive to deserve the affection of your brotherly love so far as lies within our power.

We beg you also to intercede for the peoples of the Germanic race who are given over to the worship of idols, beseeching our Lord, who gave His own blood for the salvation of the whole world and who desires that all men shall be saved and shall come to a knowledge of the truth, that He may bring them to acknowledge their Creator and lead them into the bosom of Mother Church. So also we urge you to give the aid of your prayers and to have Masses said for the souls of our brethren who labored with us in the Lord and who are now fallen asleep, and whose names the bearer of this letter will spread before you.

We earnestly pray that Your Blessedness may be well and prosperous in Christ.

XXX [40]. *Boniface arranges the affairs of the monastery of Fritzlar after the death of Abbot Wigbert* [737–738]

To his most dear sons, the priests Tatwin and Wigbert, and to Bernhard, Hiedde, Hunfrid, and Sturm, Boniface, servant of the servants of God, wishes eternal salvation in the Lord.

I call upon your affection in fatherly love to maintain the order of your monastic life the more strictly now that our father Wigbert[1] is gone. Let the priest Wigbert[2] and the deacon Megingoz expound the Rule to you. Let them have charge of the canonical hours and of the office of the Church. They are to give advice to the others, instruct the children, and preach the Word of God to the brethren. Let Hiedde be prior and rule the servants, and let Hunfrid assist him, if need be. Sturm will take charge of the kitchen. Bernhard is to be the laborer and will build our cells as

[1] Abbot of Fritzlar.
[2] A priest attached to the monastery. It seems clear that these were two different persons, but beyond that not much is known of their personalities or of their relation to some four other contemporaries of the same or a similar name. Cf. Hahn, *Bonifaz und Lul*, pp. 142 ff., 291, 319.

needed. In all matters, wherever necessary, consult Abbot Tatwin and do whatever he may direct.

Let each one of you strive with all his might to preserve his own chastity and, in your common life, to be helpful to the rest and abide in brotherly love until, God willing, I shall be with you again. Then together we will praise God and give thanks to him for all his gifts.

Farewell in Christ.

XXXI [41]. *Boniface reports to the brothers at Fritzlar and else-where his reception by Pope Gregory III*   [738]

To his beloved sons Geppan and Eoban, Tatwin and Wigbert, and all our brothers and sisters, Boniface, servant of the servants of God, sends greetings of pure affection in Christ.

Be it known to your affection—and God be thanked—that when we came safely to the threshold of St. Peter, prince of the Apostles, the apostolic pontiff received us joyfully and graciously. He gave a favorable response to our message and advised and directed us to return and continue in our established work. We are now waiting here for a council of priests and the decision of a synod, but so far we have not been informed when the apostolic pontiff will order this to be held. As soon as it is over, God willing and life permitting, we shall hasten back to you. So, now that you know this, wait for us with brotherly love and in the unity of faith, each bearing the other's burden; and so fulfilling the law of Christ, your joy shall be made full.

Farewell in Christ, and pray for us.

XXXII [42]. *Pope Gregory III commends Boniface, on his re-turn from Rome, to all bishops, priests, and abbots*   [c. 738]

Gregory, bishop and servant of the servants of God, to all our beloved bishops, reverend priests, and holy abbots of every land.

With God's help, in confirmation of His words, our brother and fellow bishop Boniface, a holy man now here present, was sent by our predecessor, Pope Gregory [II] of holy memory, into those parts to preach the word of God, and after a long time, impelled by eager desire and with God's help, he came to offer prayer at the sacred shrine of the blessed princes of the Apostles, Peter and Paul. At the conclusion of his prayers we dismissed him, under the guidance of the angel of the Lord, to the work he had begun.

May you all now be pleased to give him your friendly, respectful, and pious assistance, for the love of Christ, remembering what our Lord Jesus Christ said: "He that receiveth a prophet in the name of a prophet shall receive a prophet's reward; and he that receiveth a righteous man in the name of a righteous man shall receive a righteous man's reward." And, beloved, if perchance any one of your ministers shall wish to associate himself with this holy man in the preaching of the holy catholic faith, in no wise hinder him. Nay, rather give him your support and assign him helpers from your own flock, so that, by God's grace, there may be enough preachers of the Word to the Gentiles to win souls to God Almighty and that your community may have its share in the good work and that they be worthy to hear the Lord's voice: "You, who have left all and followed me, shall receive an hundredfold and shall inherit eternal life."

Farewell.

XXXIII [43]. *Pope Gregory III to the nobility and people of Hesse and Thuringia* [c. 738]

Pope Gregory to all the nobles and people of the German Provinces—Thuringians, Hessians, *Borthari, Nistresi, Wedreci, Lognai, Suduodi,* and *Graffelti* [Grabfeldians] and all dwellers upon the eastern bank [of the Rhine].[1]

Our predecessor, Pope Gregory of holy memory, moved by the divine spirit, dispatched the bearer of this letter, our reverend

---

[1] It is quite impossible to give English equivalents of the peoples here mentioned or even, indeed, to locate them accurately. They seem to refer to dwellers within certain regions of Hesse and Thuringia; thus the *Wedreci,* the *Lognai,* and the *Graffelti,* have been identified as the inhabitants of the Wetterau, the Lahngau, and the Grabfeld (in which Fulda was situated), respectively. The other three are not so surely identifiable.

brother and fellow bishop Boniface, to you for the perfecting of the Christian people, ordained him and instructed and guided him in the rule and system of the apostolic and catholic faith of the Roman Church, which by God's will we serve. After some time he presented himself at the threshold of the blessed princes of the Apostles to offer his devotions and asked us to expound to him whatever pertains to the salvation of souls. Then, by the divine favor, we instructed him as Holy Scripture teaches and dismissed him to return to you, beloved, enjoining upon you in the Lord to receive from him the word of exhortation and to accept the bishops and priests whom he might ordain in virtue of the apostolic authority conferred upon him, for the service of the Church. But if perchance he should find any who had wandered from the way of the true faith or the canonical teaching and should proceed against them, you were not to hinder him in any way. Whatever penalty he might impose upon them they were to accept obediently in God's name, for he who resists against obedience reaps for himself eternal damnation.

But you, my beloved, "who are baptized in the name of Christ, have put on Christ." Therefore abstain and keep yourselves from every kind of heathen practice, and not yourselves only but all who are subject to you. Reject absolutely all divination, fortune-telling, sacrifices to the dead, prophesies in groves or by fountains, amulets, incantations, sorcery (that is, wicked enchantments), and all those sacrilegious practices which used to go on in your country, and be you converted to God with your whole heart. Fear Him, reverence Him, and honor Him, bearing in mind the memory of the saints, as the Apostle says. For if thy faith, saith the Lord, shall be "as a grain of mustard seed, thou shalt say to this mountain: Come, and it cometh." Likewise our Lord God and redeemer, Jesus Christ, spoke in his sacred utterance, saying: "Thou shalt love the Lord thy God with all thy heart, and with all thy soul, and with all thy mind"; and again: "Whosoever shall confess Me before men, him will I confess also before my Father which is in heaven." And in another place he promised, saying: "And whatsoever ye shall ask my Father in my name, that will I do"; and similarly: "Ask, and it shall be given you; seek and ye shall find; knock and it shall be opened unto you. For everyone that asketh receiveth; and he that seeketh findeth, and to him that knocketh it shall be opened." Do you therefore, dearly beloved, bring forth fruits meet for repentance, that in the day of the coming of our Lord Jesus Christ you may be worthy to receive mansions in heaven.

Farewell.

XXXIV [44]. *Pope Gregory III to the bishops in Bavaria and Alemannia*   [c. 738]

Pope Gregory to our beloved bishops in the province of Bavaria and Alemannia: Wigo, Liudo, Rydolt, Vivilo, and Adda.

Catholic authority, as well as that of the holy fathers, directs that twice in every year a synod should be held for the welfare of the Christian people and the edification of the sons of the adoption, together with a trial of canonical cases, so that the interests of everyone may be furthered according to his need. Wherefore I urge and command you, beloved, by the mercy of God, that "ye walk worthy of the vocation wherewith ye are called," that your ministry may be perfect before God.

It is well for you to understand that you are to receive our fellow bishop Boniface now here with us, as our representative and vicar with due and appropriate honors, in the name of Christ. You are to accept from him and worthily maintain the service of the Church and the catholic faith according to the form and usage of the Holy Catholic and Apostolic Church of God, over which we preside by the mercy of God, as he is commissioned by us with apostolic authority. The practices and doctrines of the heathen, of Britons who come to you, of false, heretical, and adulterous priests wheresoever they may come from, you are to reject, prohibit, and cast away from you. The people entrusted to you by God you are to instruct with kindly admonition and turn them absolutely away from sacrifices to the dead. According to the teaching of our afore-mentioned fellow priest, make haste so to hold fast the catholic and apostolic faith as to please the Lord our God and Savior. To whatever place he shall call you to assemble in council, whether near the Danube or in the city of Augsburg or wherever he may direct, there be ready to go in Christ's name, so that we may learn through his report of your assembly, that in the day of the coming of Christ Jesus you may be worthy to stand before his judgment seat with the fruits of your good works, saying: "Lo, here are we and the children thou hast given us; we have not lost a single one of them," and to hear the Lord's voice: "Come, ye blessed of my Father, inherit the kingdom prepared for you from the foundation of the world."

Farewell.

XXXV [45]. *Pope Gregory III to Boniface. Organization of the Church in Bavaria*   Oct. 29, 739

Gregory, servant of the servants of God, to Boniface, his reverend and holy brother and fellow bishop.

The teacher of all nations, the eminent Apostle Paul spoke, saying: "All things work together for good to them that love God." When we learned from your report that God in His mercy had deigned to set free so many in Germany from the power of the heathen and had brought as many as a hundred thousand souls into the bosom of Mother Church through your efforts and those of Charles, prince of the Franks, and when we heard what you had accomplished in Bavaria, we lifted up our hands to heaven in thanks to the Lord our God, giver of all good, who opened the gates of mercy and loving-kindness in those western lands for the knowledge of the way of salvation and sent his angel to prepare the way before you. Glory be to Him forever and ever!

You inform us that you have visited the Bavarian people and found that they were not living in accordance with the prescriptions of the Church, that there was but one bishop in that province, a certain Uiuilo [Wilhelm?] whom we ordained a long time ago, and that you have, with the approval of Odilo, duke of those same Bavarians, and of the nobles of that province, ordained three other bishops. You have also divided the province into four districts, so that each bishop may have his own diocese. In all this you have acted well and wisely, my brother, since you have fulfilled the apostolic precepts in our stead and have done as we directed you. Cease not therefore, most reverend brother, to teach them the holy catholic and apostolic tradition of the Roman See, that the natives may be enlightened and may follow in the way of salvation and so may gain eternal reward.

As to the priests whom you have found there: if those who ordained them are unknown and it is uncertain whether they were bishops or not, if the priests are catholic men and of good repute, trained in the service of Christ, well versed in the whole sacred law, and fitted for their office, then let each receive from his bishop the priestly benediction and consecration and so perform the duties of his sacred office.

It is advisable that those who were baptized according to the varieties and the inflections of the heathen dialects, provided they were baptized in the name of the Trinity, should be confirmed with the sacred chrism and the laying on of hands.

Bishop Uiuilo was ordained by ourself. If, then, he has in any way gone beyond the canonical rule, instruct and correct him according to the tradition of the Roman Church as you received it from us.

In regard to a council which you are to hold in the Danube valley in our stead: we direct Your Fraternity to be present there vested with apostolic authority. In so far as God shall give you strength, cease not to preach the Word of Salvation that the faith of Christ may increase and multiply in the name of God.

You are not at liberty, my brother, to linger in one place when your work there is done; but strengthen the hearts of the brethren and of all the faithful throughout those regions of the West, and wherever God shall open to you a way to save souls, carry on your preaching. Wherever you may find places in need of bishops, ordain them in our stead according to the canonical rule and teach them to observe the apostolic and canonical tradition. For so you will prepare great rewards for yourself, because you will gain for our God Almighty a well-instructed and devout people. Shrink not, beloved brother, from hard and long journeys, that the Christian faith may be spread far and wide through your exertions; for it is written: "Strait and narrow is the way that leadeth unto life." Carry on, therefore, my brother, the good work you have begun, so that in the day of Christ our God you can speak in the assembly of the saints about to be judged saying: "Lo, here am I and the children thou hast given me; I have not lost a single one of them." And again: "Lord thou gavest unto me five talents: behold, I have gained other five also." Then shall you be worthy to hear the voice of God saying: "Well done, thou good and faithful servant: Thou hast been faithful over a few things, I will make thee ruler over many things: Enter thou into the joy of thy lord."

God keep you in safety, most reverend brother.

Given on the fourth day before the Kalends of November on the twenty-third year of our most pious and august Lord Leo by God crowned emperor, on the twenty-third year of his consulship and the twentieth year of the Emperor Constantine his son, in the eighth indiction.

XXXVI [46]. *Boniface calls upon all Anglo-Saxons to pray for the conversion of the Saxons* [c. 738]

To all his reverend fellow bishops, to all those clothed with the grace of priesthood, deacons, canons, clerks, abbots, and abbesses set over the true flock of Christ, monks living in humble submission to God, virgins consecrated by vows to God, and all consecrated handmaids of Christ—and, in general, to all God-fearing catholics of the stock and race of the Angles, Boniface named also Winfred, born of that same race, German legate of the Church Universal, servant of the Apostolic See and called Archbishop for no merit of his own, sends greetings of humble communion and unfeigned love in Christ.

We earnestly beseech your brotherly goodness to be mindful of us, who are worth so little, in your prayers that we may be delivered from the snare of Satan the huntsman and from wicked and cruel men, that the word of God may make its way and be glorified. We beseech you to obtain through your holy prayers, that our Lord and God Jesus Christ, "who will have all men to be saved, and to come unto the knowledge of God," may turn the hearts of the pagan Saxons to the catholic faith, that they may free themselves from the snares of the devil in which they are bound and may be gathered among the children of Mother Church.

Take pity upon them; for they themselves are saying: "We are of one blood and one bone with you." Remember that the way of all the earth is at hand and that in hell no one will confess God, nor will death praise him.

Know also that in making this request I have the approval, the consent, and the blessing of two pontiffs of the Roman Church. Act now upon this our supplication so that your reward may shine with increasing splendor in the heavenly house of the angels.

May the Omnipotent Creator always keep the unity and communion of your affection in power and progress in Christ.

XXXVII [47]. *Bishop Torthelm of Leicester to Boniface regarding the conversion of the Saxons* [After 737]

To my most dearly beloved master, abounding in the spirit of charity and especially in the grace of God and ever ruling in Christ his flock with pastoral care, Archbishop Boniface, called also Winfred, Torthelm, bishop and servant of the servants of God, sends greeting in the Lord.

We have received the welcome letter of Your Excellency and as we read it we felt your most loyal devotion and fervent love toward the holy life, so that your thoughts dwell day and night, under the protecting hand of God, upon the conversion of the pagan Saxons to the catholic and apostolic faith for the redemption of your own soul. Who would not rejoice to hear these pleasant things? Who would not exult and be glad at such accomplishments, whereby people of our own race are coming to believe in Christ the Almighty God?

I am sending you by the bearer of your letter a gift, small indeed, but token of a great affection. It is also a pledge that we most gladly undertake to do all that you have been pleased to ask of our insignificance, namely that we would bear Your Holiness in mind in the celebration of Mass and in our daily prayers. And, conscious of our own frailty, we earnestly pray you to do the same on your part, and this you can do more satisfactorily than we, as your merits surpass ours. May Your Eminence therefore hasten to gather in and dedicate this new people to Christ, enjoying as you do the protection of our Lord Jesus Christ, Redeemer of the human race.

And so, greeting Your Excellency with fraternal affection, we earnestly beseech divine mercy to aid you and all yours in all good works, that you may reign with Christ in the world to come.

XXXVIII [48]. *Boniface seeks protection for his mission in Thuringia from the palace mayor, Grifo*   [741]

Boniface, servant of the servants of God, sends greeting in Christ to Grifo, son of Charles.

I beg and beseech your favor in the name of God the Father Almighty and Jesus Christ His Son and the Holy Spirit, by the Holy Trinity and the Unity of God, that if God gives you the power, you will aid the servants of God in Thuringia, clerks, priests, monks, and handmaidens of Christ, and will defend the Christian people against the malice of the heathen, that the pagans may not destroy them and that you may have your eternal reward before the judgment seat of Christ. Be assured that we bear you in mind before God, as your father, during his lifetime, and your mother also desired me to do. We pray God, the Savior of the world, to guide your way in life to the salvation of your soul, that you may abide in the grace of God now and forevermore.

Meanwhile, remember, my dear sons, the word of the Psalmist: "As for man, his days are as grass: as a flower of the field, so he flourisheth." And the Apostle says: "The whole world lieth in wickedness." And the Truth says in the Gospel: "What shall it profit a man if he shall gain the whole world, and lose his own soul?" And again in the Gospel, of the glory of the just: "Then shall the righteous shine forth as the sun, in the kingdom of their Father." And Paul the Apostle concerning the blessedness of the eternal life: "Eye hath not seen, nor ear heard, neither have entered into the heart of man, the things which God hath prepared for them that love him."

Act therefore, my sons, so that your reward may shine ever more brightly in the highest heaven.

We pray that it may be well with you for length of days in Christ.

XXXIX [49]. *Denehard, Lullus, and Burchard to Abbess Cuniburg asking her prayers for help* [739–741]

To their beloved lady, most devoted to Christ, Abbess Cuniburg, eminent for the nobility of her royal blood, her sons and fellow countrymen Denehard, Lullus, and Burchard send wishes for her eternal welfare.

Holding you of all women in the innermost chamber of our hearts we desire your gracious kindness to know that, after the death of our parents and our other relatives, we went over to the people of Germany, were received into the monastic rule of the venerable archbishop, Boniface, and have become his assistants in his work in so far as our humble incapacity permits.

And now, we beseech you from the depths of our hearts that you will be pleased to keep us in communion with your holy congregation, and with the support of your prayers guide our little bark, worn out by the tempests of this world, into safe harbor, and that you will not refuse to shelter us against the cruel darts of sin with the shield of your prayer, as we also pray the divine aid every moment for the welfare of Your Eminence. If we were actually present before you on bended knee and with floods of tears, we trust that our request would be granted; so now, in our absence, we humbly beg the same favor from you. We also wish it known to your care and your wisdom that if any one of us should happen to visit Britain we should not prefer the obedience and government of any man to subjection under your good-will; for we place the greatest confidence of our hearts in you.

We beg also that you will send on by the bearer of this letter two young freedmen, named Begiloc and Man, whom I, Lullus, and my father released at our departure for Rome and entrusted to my uncle for the welfare of my soul—if this should be their free act and if they are within your jurisdiction. And if any one shall unlawfully try to prevent their journey we beg you to protect them.

Some little gifts accompany this letter: frankincense, pepper, and cinnamon—a very small present, but given out of heartfelt affection. We pray you not to think of the size of the gift but to remember the loving spirit. We beg you also to correct this unlearned letter and to send a few of your own sweet words, which we shall eagerly await.

Farewell, and may you live long and happily to make intercession for us.

XL [50]. *Boniface to Pope Zacharias on his accession to the papacy*
[Early in 742]

To our best beloved Lord Zacharias, the apostolic man wearing the insignia of the supreme pontificate, Boniface, a servant of the servants of God.

We must confess, our father and lord, that after we learned from messengers that your predecessor in the apostolate, Gregory of reverend memory, pontiff of the Apostolic See, had been set free from the prison of the body and had passed on to God, nothing gave us greater joy or happiness than the knowledge that the Supreme Arbiter had appointed your fatherly clemency to administer the canon law and to govern the Apostolic See. We gave thanks to God with uplifted hands. And so, just as if we were kneeling at your feet, we most earnestly pray that, as we have been devoted servants and willing disciples of your predecessors under the authority of St. Peter, so also we may be worthy to be the obedient servants of Your Holiness under the canon law. It is our earnest desire to maintain the catholic faith and the unity of the Roman Church. As many hearers or learners as God shall grant me in my missionary work, I will not cease to summon and urge them to render obedience to the Apostolic See.

We have also to inform Your Paternity that by the grace of God we have appointed three bishops over those peoples in Germany who have been to a certain extent won over and converted and we have divided the province into three dioceses. The bishoprics of these three towns or cities where they were ordained we beg you to confirm and establish by your authority in writing. We have appointed one episcopal see in the fortress called Würzburg, another in the town of Buraburg, and a third in a place called Erfurt, which was formerly a city of heathen rustics. The choice of these three places we earnestly pray you to strengthen and confirm by your own charter and by authority of your apostolic office, so that, God willing, there may be in Germany three episcopal sees founded and established by apostolic order and under the authority and direction of St. Peter. And may neither the present nor any future generation presume to break up these dioceses or to defy the orders of the Apostolic See.

Be it known also to Your Paternity that Karlmann, duke of the Franks, summoned me to him and requested me to bring together a council in the part of the Frankish kingdom which is under his rule. He promised that he would do something toward reforming and reëstablishing the ecclesiastical discipline, which for a long time, not less than sixty or seventy years, has been despoiled and trampled upon. If, therefore, he is really willing, under divine inspiration, to carry out this purpose, I should have the advice and direction of your authority—that is, the authority of the Apostolic See. The Franks, according to their elders, have not held a council for more than eighty years, nor have they had an archbishop or established or restored anywhere the canon law of the Church. For the most part the episcopal sees in cities are in the hands of greedy laymen or are exploited by adulterous and vicious clergymen and publicans for secular uses. If, then, I am to undertake this business by your orders and at the instance of the aforesaid duke, I desire to have at once the command and the suggestions of the Apostolic See, together with the Church canons.

If I find among these men certain so-called deacons who have spent their lives since boyhood in debauchery, adultery, and every kind of filthiness, who entered the diaconate with this reputation, and who now, while they have four or five concubines in their beds, still read the Gospel and are not ashamed or afraid to call themselves deacons—nay rather, entering upon the priesthood, they continue in the same vices, add sin to sin, declare that they have a right to make intercession for the people in the priestly office and to celebrate Mass, and, still worse, with such reputations advancing from step to step to nomination and appointment as bishops—may I have the formal prescription of your authority as to your procedure in such cases so that they may be convicted by an apostolic judgment and dealt with as sinners? And certain bishops are to be found among them who, although they deny that they are fornicators or adulterers, are drunkards and shiftless men, given to hunting and to fighting in the army like soldiers and by their own hands shedding blood, whether of heathens or Christians. Since I am the recognized servant and legate of the Apostolic See, my word here and your word there ought to agree, in case I should send messengers, as I have done in the past, to learn the decision of your authority.[1]

In another matter, also, I have to ask your advice and permission. Your predecessor of reverend memory directed me in your presence, to name, God willing, a [certain] priest as my heir and successor in the service of the Church in case of my death. If this be the will of God, it is agreeable to me. But now I am in doubt and do not know whether it can be done, because since then a brother of that priest has killed an uncle of the duke of the Franks and up to the present time we do not know how and when that quarrel will be settled. I pray you, therefore, to give me your

---

[1] The text seems obviously corrupt, but this appears to be the meaning.

authority to act in this choice, with the approval of the servants of
God, as may seem best to us all for God and for the advantage and
spiritual profit of the Church and the protection of religion. May
I have your consent to act in this matter as God shall deign to
inspire me, since it does not seem possible to accomplish it against
the wishes of the prince?

I have further to seek the advice of Your Paternity in regard
to a certain perplexing and scandalous report which has come to us
recently and has greatly disturbed us, filling with confusion the
priests of our churches. A certain layman of high station came to us
and said that Gregory of sainted memory, pontiff of the Apostolic
See, had granted him permission to marry the widow of his uncle.
She had formerly been the wife of her own cousin but had left him
during his lifetime. She is known to be related in the third degree
to the man who now desires her and who declares that permission
was granted him. She formerly made a vow of chastity before
God and took the veil but laid it aside and was married.

The aforesaid man declares that he has a license from the
Apostolic See for such a marriage as this! But we do not believe
this to be true; for a synod of the church of the Saxons beyond
the sea, in which I was born and reared, namely the synod of
London [605], convoked and directed by disciples of St. Gregory,
the archbishops—Augustine, Laurentius, Justus, and Miletus—declared such a marriage union, on the authority of Holy Scripture,
to be a heinous crime, an incestuous and horrible offense, and a
damnable sin. Wherefore, I beg Your Paternity to deign to enlighten us as to the true doctrine in this case, that scandals and
schisms or new errors may not arise and increase therefrom among
the clergy and the Christian people.

Some of the ignorant common people, Alemanians, Bavarians,
and Franks, hearing that many of the offenses prohibited by us
are practiced in the city of Rome imagine that they are allowed by
the priests there and reproach us for causing them to incur blame
in their own lives. They say that on the first day of January year
after year, in the city of Rome and in the neighborhood of St.

Peter's church by day or night, they have seen bands of singers parading the streets in pagan fashion, shouting and chanting sacrilegious songs and loading tables with food day and night, while no one in his own house is willing to lend his neighbor fire or tools or any other convenience. They say also that they have seen there women with amulets and bracelets of heathen fashion on their arms and legs, offering them for sale to willing buyers. All these things, seen by evil-minded and ignorant people, are a cause of reproach to us and a hindrance to our preaching and teaching. It is of such things that the Apostle says reprovingly: "Ye observe days and times; I fear I have labored with you in vain." And St. Augustine said:

He who believes in such evil things, as incantations or diviners or soothsayers, or amulets, or any kind of prophesies, even though he fast, or pray, or run to church continually, and though he give alms generously, or torment his body with all kinds of tortures, it shall profit him nothing so long as he does not abandon these sacrilegious rites.

If Your Paternity would prohibit these heathen practices at Rome, it would bring rewards to you and the greatest advantage to us in our teaching.

Some bishops and priests of the Frankish nation who were adulterers and fornicators of the worst kind, whose children born during their episcopate or priesthood bear witness against them, now declare, on returning from the Apostolic See, that the Roman Pontiff has given them permission to carry on their episcopal service in the Church. Against this we maintain that we have never heard that the Apostolic See had ever given a decision contrary to canonical decrees.

All these things, beloved master, we make known to you that we may give an answer to these people upon your authority and that under guidance of your instruction the sheep of the Church may not be led astray and that the ravening wolves may be overcome and destroyed.

We are sending you some trifling gifts, not as being worthy of Your Paternity, but as a token of our affection and our devoted obedience, a warm rug and a little silver and gold.

May God's hand protect your Holiness and may you have health and length of days in Christ.

May God enthroned on High for long preserve
In His holy Temple the ruler of the Apostolic See,
   May the honey-sweet doctrine visit the grateful earth
And make it worthy of God for Christ's blessed sake,
   May the blooming Mother rejoice,
And may the House of the Lord be joyful with abundant offering!

XLI [51]. *Answers of Pope Zacharias to the inquiries of Boniface*
April 1, 743

Zacharias, servant of the servants of God, to his very reverend and holy brother and fellow bishop, Boniface.

From your letter, most holy brother, brought to us by your pious priest Denehard, we learn that you are in good health, as we hope you may always be, and we have rendered earnest thanks to our Almighty and Merciful God, who has deigned to prosper you in all good works. You fill our heart with exceeding joy whenever letters of Your Holiness come to us and we find there what pertains to the salvation of souls—how new peoples are daily brought into the bosom of our Holy Mother Church through your preaching.

We learn there also that you have established three bishops in three several places who are to preside over the people whom the Lord God has deigned to bring over to himself by means of Your Holiness. You ask that these episcopal sees may be established by our authority; but let Your Fraternity give further thought and examine most carefully whether this is advisable, whether the places and the number of inhabitants are worthy of having bishops. You remember, beloved, what is laid down in the sacred canons: that we should not establish bishops in villages or small cities, lest the title bishop be cheapened.

However, we are moved by your earnest and appealing letter to grant your request without delay. We ordain by apostolic authority that episcopal sees be established there, worthy to have a line of bishops who shall preside over the people and carry the word of preaching to their subjects—namely, one in the fortress called Würzburg, a second in the town of Buraburg, and a third in the place called Erfurt—and let no one whosoever dare henceforth violate what we have thus established and confirmed by authority of the Blessed Apostle Peter.

You inform us that our son Karlmann summoned you to meet him and arrange for a synod to be held in that part of the Frankish kingdom subject to his rule, since all church regulations have been completely destroyed in that province, a fact greatly to be regretted. For a long time no assembly of priests has been held there, and in consequence those who call themselves priests do not even know what priesthood is. When however, by God's help, the promises of our afore-mentioned son have been fulfilled and Your Fraternity shall have taken your place in council with that most eminent man, then, if you find bishops, priests, or deacons who are violating the canons or the rules of the fathers—that is, living in adultery or having more than one wife, or if they have shed the blood of Christians or pagans, or if Your Holiness shall find that they have acted contrary to any other requirements—you shall on no account permit them to perform the duties of priests by apostolic authority; for such persons are condemned out of their own mouths as false priests and are known to be worse than laymen, being lustful and bound in infamous unions and having their hands stained with human blood. How can they believe themselves to be priests, or what do they think of God's word: "Let my priests marry once," and the words of the Apostle, "husband of one wife," et cetera. And this is lawful only before entering the priesthood; for after that they are prohibited from a regular marriage. How do they think they can serve as priests who show themselves to be involved in such crimes as we should not allow pious laymen to be entangled? How dare they touch the sacred mysteries, or offer prayers for the sins of the people, when the sacred canons prescribe that not even a simple clerk not in priestly order may enter into a second marriage? These men, on the other hand, commit sins worse than those of laymen not only by refusing to abstain from one wife after their ordination but by daring to take more than one, when not even one is permitted.

Regarding all this as a matter of little importance and calling down upon themselves the wrath of God, they commit still greater crimes by slaying Christians and pagans with their own hands; so that those on whom, for the remission of sins, they are duty bound to pour the water of baptism and to whom they are bound to administer the sacraments of Christ are, on the contrary, killed by their sacrilegious hands. But how can any reasoning mind regard as priests those who neither abstain from lust nor keep their hands clean of blood? Or who can think that their offerings are acceptable to God, when, as the Prophet says: "The Lord will abhor the bloody and deceitful man." So, as I have said before, we command you not to suffer them to perform the priestly functions or to deal with the sacred mysteries. In whatever other respects you may find that they have acted contrary to the rules of the Church, keep the canons and the ordinances of the fathers ready at hand and make your decisions according to what you find there.

You say that you are entitled to name your successor and that a bishop may be chosen in your place while you are still living; but we cannot permit this under any consideration whatsoever. It is manifestly contrary to every rule of the Church and the opinions of the fathers. It is our will that you have an assistant in preaching the Gospel of Christ, according to the word of the Apostle: "Whoso shall have done good service, shall purchase to himself a good degree." It would obviously be a detestable fault for us to appoint a substitute for you during your own life. We order you, so long as divine mercy may permit you to live, to offer up prayer without ceasing that God may grant you a successor who will be pleasing to Him and who may be able to govern without reproach the people whom God has seen fit to bring to His grace through the efforts of Your Holiness and lead them into the way of life. For how could we grant this request of yours, even if we desired to do so, seeing that we are but frail mortals, ignorant of what the coming day may bring forth and unable to say which one of us may be the first to depart this life? However, if it shall please the divine mercy that he shall outlive you, and if you have found him to be a suitable person and you have quite made up your mind, then, as soon as you are conscious that you are about to depart this life, in the presence of all [the people] designate your successor and let him come hither for his consecration. But this privilege which we have thought proper to grant you out of our affection for you, we cannot permit to be conferred upon any other person.

As to the man who wishes to marry his uncle's widow, who was formerly the wife of her own cousin and who is proved to have taken the sacred veil, and has spread abroad the story that our predecessor of blessed memory granted him license to take her in this scandalous marriage—God forbid that our predecessor should have ordered such a thing! The Apostolic See never orders anything contrary to the prescriptions of the fathers or of the canons. Cease not, beloved brother, to warn them, exhort them, and urge upon them to refrain from such an abominable union lest they perish eternally. Let them remember that they are redeemed by the blood of Christ and not deliver themselves of their own will into the power of the devil by this incestuous marriage but rather give themselves to that God and Christ His Son and that Holy Spirit in whose name they have been snatched from the power of that ancient foe. Impress upon them, most holy brother, the word of Scripture: "Let him know, that he which converteth the sinner from the error of his way shall save a soul from death, and shall hide a multitude of sins." We, too, have sent him a word of warning in this case.

In regard to the New Year celebrations, auguries, amulets, incantations, and other practices which you say are observed after heathen fashion at the church of St. Peter the Apostle or in the city of Rome, we hold them to be wrong and pernicious for us and for all Christians, according to God's word: "Neither shall ye use enchantment, nor observe times." And again Scripture says: "Surely there is no enchantment against Jacob, neither is there any divination against Israel." So also we think we should be on our guard and not pay any attention to auguries and divinations; for we have been taught that all such things were repudiated by the fathers. And because they were cropping out again, we have abolished them all from the day when divine favor ordered us, unworthy as we are, to act in place of the Apostle. In the same way we desire you to teach the people subject to you and so to lead them in the way of eternal life. All these practices were prohibited loyally and faithfully by a decree of our predecessor and teacher, Gregory of sacred memory, and also many others which, at the instigation of the devil, were cropping up in the sheepfold of Christ. We hasten to follow his example for the salvation of that people.

As to those priests who hold false doctrines or are proven adulterers or fornicators and say that they received indulgence and license to preach from the Apostolic See, let not Your Fraternity put any faith in them at all, but inflict the canonical punishment on them in the same way as on those about whom we gave instructions above. We desire you to act only according to the sacred canons or the instructions of the Apostolic See.

In accordance with the request of Your Holiness we are sending separate letters of confirmation for your three bishops, asking you to deliver them with your own hand.

To our son Karlmann we have also sent letters urging him to fulfill immediately his promises to you and to lend you his aid.

Such, beloved brother, are our answers to the inquiries above enumerated, as the Lord has prompted us, for the abolition of all those scandals of diabolical fraud. If other disorders occur, strive to correct them among the people entrusted to you, as the sacred canons direct. It is not right for us to preach otherwise than as we are taught by the holy fathers; but if through the wiles of our ancient foe some new situation should arise which you could not solve by the provisions of the sacred canons, do not hesitate to refer it to us, so that, with God's help, we may hasten without delay to make such answer as may be for the welfare of that new people.

Be assured, dearest brother, that you hold so firm a place in our affections that we would gladly have you near us daily in close companionship, as a minister of God and steward of the churches of Christ.

Finally, beloved brother, have comfort in God, be brave and strong in the work to which divine mercy has called you; for that great hope of reward awaits you which God has promised to those who love Him. And we, sinner that we are, will never cease to implore the boundless grace of our God, that "he who has begun a good work in you may perform it" to the end. And may the blessed Peter, prince of the apostles, labor with you in all good things which you do in obedience to him and according to your desire.

May God keep you in safety, most reverend and holy father.

Given on the Kalends of April in the twenty-fourth year of our most pious and august Lord Constantine, by God crowned emperor, in the second year of his consulship, in the eleventh indiction.

XLII [52]. *Pope Zacharias confirms the establishment of the bishopric of Buraburg* April 1, 743

Pope Zacharias to our best beloved Wintan, [bishop] of the holy church of Buraburg.

Our most holy and reverend brother and fellow bishop Boniface informs us that, with God's help and support in spreading abroad the Christian law and the way of the orthodox faith, according to the teaching of this Holy Roman Church over which we preside by the ordinance of God, he established episcopal sees in that part of Germany where you have control and has divided the province into three dioceses.[1] When we heard this we lifted up our hands to heaven in triumph and gave thanks to the Enlightener and Giver of All Good, the Lord our God and our Savior Jesus Christ, "who maketh both one."

[1] The regular use of the plural address shows that this letter was a circular sent to each of the three newly ordained German bishops. An identical letter, addressed to the bishop of Würzburg, follows. It is not here translated.

The aforesaid holy man further besought us in his letter to confirm your appointment by our apostolic authority. Wherefore, we most willingly with divine assistance and by authority of the blessed Peter, prince of the Apostles, to whom was given by God and our Savior Jesus Christ power to bind and loose the sins of men in heaven and upon earth, do confirm your episcopal sees and decree that they shall remain fixed for all time. We forbid, by authority of the same prince of the Apostles, that any person shall dare to act counter to your episcopal jurisdicition granted you by our order and by God's favor. We forbid also, according to the tradition of the sacred canons, that any bishop shall dare to occupy your see by being transferred from another bishopric or that anyone, except the representative of our Apostolic See in those parts, shall appoint the new bishop after you shall have been called from this world. On the other hand, let no one of you venture to invade the diocese of another or draw away churches therefrom. If any one of you—which God forbid!—shall with rash presumption, act contrary to this our command, let him know that he will be bound in the chains of anathema by the eternal judgment of God. But whoso shall keep the apostolic precepts and maintain the standard of the true orthodox faith shall receive the grace of benediction. We implore the divine favor to confirm and strengthen what God has wrought in you; and may the love of God, His grace, and His peace be with your souls, my best beloved and most holy brethren. Labor with all your might for the faith of Christ, and strive to carry on his service so that you may be worthy to say with the great Apostle: "I have fought a good fight, I have finished my course, I have kept the faith: Henceforth there is laid up for me a crown of righteousness, which the Lord, the righteous judge, shall give me at that day."

We salute you in the Lord and pray that it may be well with you. Farewell.

Given on the Kalends of April, in the twenty-fourth year of our most pious and august Lord Constantine, by God crowned emperor, in the second year of his consulship, in the eleventh indiction.

XLIII [54]. *Cardinal-Deacon Gemmulus to Boniface: apology for delay in sending a copy of the* Registrum *of Pope Gregory I* [742–743]

To the most holy and excellent and beloved father, Boniface, archbishop of the province of Germany, Gemmulus, unworthy deacon of the Holy Apostolic See.

This will inform you that the consoling letter sent by Your Holy Paternity and brought by your messenger Denehard, a venerable man, was received with all due respect and affection; also the blessing which you sent me. It was more precious to me than silver or gold, because I saw in it the gracious evidence that I was remembered in your holy prayers. May divine majesty preserve you to me in good health, so long as grace from on high shall suffer me to live, so that, aided by your holy intercession, I may be found the better equipped by God's favor to fight against the assaults of our ancient foe.

You have asked me to send you some of the Epistles of St. Gregory; but thus far we have been unable to obey your command. I have been sadly afflicted with a painful gouty complaint, as your afore-mentioned priest has long known, so that he had to leave me still suffering. He will explain all to you by word of mouth. But if life permit and your prayers do not fail, as soon as I am restored to health I shall fulfill the commands of Your Holy Paternity. The next time you send your messenger hither your requests shall be met and your wishes fulfilled without delay. We are sending by your aforesaid priest some *cozumber* of a marvelous fragrant odor, which you may offer as incense to God at matins or vespers or at the celebration of Mass; and I beg you to accept without offense what is offered out of pure affection, saluting you, holy father, in the Lord and asking you to pray for us. I salute the whole congregation that is with you and ask for their prayers. "The earnest prayer of the righteous man availeth much." And I, too, sinner though I be, am instant in prayer for you before the shrines of the Apostles. We wish Your Holy Paternity good health in the Lord. May divine majesty increase and prosper the work you have undertaken and cause it ever to bring forth more fruit.

May the Indivisible Trinity preserve Your Holiness in prayer for us.

XLIV [56]. *Karlmann, palace mayor of the Eastern Franks, publishes the decrees of the synods of 742 and 743*

In the name of our Lord Jesus Christ. I, Karlmann, duke and prince of the Franks, in the seven hundred and forty-second year of the Incarnation of Christ and the twenty-first day of April, by the advice of the servants of God and my chief men, have brought together in the fear of Christ the bishops of my realm with their priests into a council or synod; namely, Archbishop Boniface, Burchard [Würzburg], Reginfried [Cologne], Wintan [Buraburg], Willibald [Erfurt?], Dadanus [Utrecht or Erfurt], and Eddanus [Strasburg], together with their priests, that they might give me their advice how the law of God and the service of religion, fallen into decay under former princes, might be reëstablished, and how the Christian people might attain salvation for their souls and not perish through the deceit of false priests.

And, by the advice of my priests and nobles we have appointed bishops for the several cities and have set over them as archbishop Boniface, the delegate of St. Peter.

We have ordered that a synod shall be held every year, so that in our presence the canonical decrees and the laws of the Church may be reëstablished and the Christian religion purified.

Revenues, of which churches were defrauded, we have restored and given back to them. We have deprived false priests and adulterous or lustful deacons of their church incomes, have degraded them, and forced them to do penance.

We have absolutely forbidden the servants of God to carry arms or fight, to enter the army or march against an enemy, except only so many as are especially selected for divine service such as celebrating Mass or carrying relics—that is to say: the prince may have one or two bishops with the chaplains, and each prefect one priest to hear confessions and prescribe penance. We have also forbidden the servants of God to hunt or wander about the woods with dogs or to keep hawks and falcons.

We have also ordered, according to the sacred canons, that every priest living within a diocese shall be subject to the bishop of that diocese. Annually during Lent he shall render to the bishop an account of his ministry, in regard to baptism in the catholic faith, to prayers, and the order of the Mass. Whenever, according to the canon law, the bishop shall make the rounds of his diocese for the purpose of confirmation, the priest is to be ready to receive him with those who are going to be confirmed already assembled and coöperating. On Holy Thursday let him ask the bishop for fresh consecrated oil and bear witness before the bishop of his chastity, his way of life, and his belief.

We have ordered, according to canonical warning, that unknown bishops and priests, wherever they may come from, shall not be admitted into the service of the Church until they shall be approved by the synod.

We have decreed, according to the canons, that every bishop within his own diocese and with the help of the count, who is the defender of the Church, shall see to it that the people of God perform no pagan rites but reject and cast out all the foulness of the heathen, such as sacrifices to the dead, casting of lots, divinations, amulets and auguries, incantations, or offerings of animals, which foolish folk perform in the churches, according to pagan custom, in the name of holy martyrs or confessors, thereby calling down the wrath of God and his saints, and also those sacrilegious fires which they call "Niedfeor," and whatever other pagan practices there may be.

We have further ordered that after this synod held on April the twenty-first, any of the servants of God or the maids of Christ falling into carnal sin shall do penance in prison on bread and water. If it be an ordained priest he shall be imprisoned for two years, first flogged to bleeding and afterward further disciplined at the bishop's discretion. But if a clerk or monk fall into this sin, after a third flogging he shall be imprisoned for a year and there do penance. Likewise a veiled nun shall be bound to do the same penance, and all her hair shall be shaved.

We have decreed also that priests and deacons shall not wear cloaks after the fashion of laymen, but cassocks according to the usage of the servants of God. Let no priest or deacon permit a woman to live in the same house with him. Let cloistered monks and maids of God live after the Rule of St. Benedict and govern their lives accordingly.

THE SECOND SYNOD

And now, in this synodal assembly, called for the first day of March in the place called Leptines, all the venerable priests of God, the counts and prefects have accepted and confirmed the decrees of the former synod and have promised to carry them out and observe them.

The whole body of the clergy—bishops, priests, deacons, and clerks—accepting the canons of the ancient fathers, have promised to restore the laws of the Church as to morals and doctrine and form of service. Abbots and monks have accepted the Rule of the holy father, Benedict, for the reformation of the regular life.

We order that corrupt and adulterous clerics who have defiled the holy places and monasteries by occupying them until now shall be expelled and made to do penance, and if, after this declaration, they fall into the crime of fornication or adultery they shall suffer the penalties prescribed at the former synod. The same with monks and nuns.

We order also, by the advice of the servants of God and of the Christian people and in view of imminent wars and attacks by the foreign populations which surround us, that a portion of the properties of the Church shall be used for some time longer, with God's indulgence, for the benefit of our army, as a *precarium* and paying a *census*, on condition, however, that annually from each *casata* [of these ecclesiastical estates] one *solidus*, that is twelve *denarii*, shall be paid to the church or monastery which owns it. In case of the death of the persons to whom the property was entrusted as a *precarium*, it shall revert to the Church. Also, if conditions are such that the prince deems it necessary, let the *precarium* be renewed for another term and a new contract be written. But let extreme care be taken that churches and monasteries whose property is granted in *precarium* shall not be reduced to poverty and suffer want; and, if they should thus be distressed, let the whole property be given back to the church and the house of God.[1]

We likewise ordain that, in accordance with the canonical decrees, adultery and incestuous marriages contrary to law shall be forbidden and shall be punished at the discretion of the bishop. And let not Christian slaves be transferred to pagans.

We have also decreed, as my father [Charles Martel] did before me, that whosoever engages in heathen practices of any sort shall be condemned to pay a fine of fifteen *solidi*.

XLV [57]. *Pope Zacharias to Boniface in regard to the grant of the pallium to the archbishops of Rouen, Rheims, and Sens*
June 22, 744

Zacharias to his very reverend and holy brother, Boniface.

We read in the book of the Acts of the Apostles that the Holy Spirit commanded the Apostles saying: "Separate me Barnabas and Saul for the work whereunto I have called them," i.e., that through the preaching of the Christian religion and the grace of that same Holy Spirit they might enlighten the whole world. Through the light of their preaching and of the teaching of Christ the universal Church of God has stood and still stands shining forth in the splendor of their doctrine and that of the blessed Peter, prince of the Apostles.

It is our belief that you, most holy brother, have likewise been chosen by divine inspiration to follow in their footsteps in those lands and that the same Holy Spirit has called you to the same work of enlightenment for those peoples. Wherefore we rejoice greatly in God and return unbounded thanks to His almighty power. When your several letters were read to us in detail, we

[1] See A. Bondroit, "Les *precariae verbo regis* avant le concile de Leptinnes," in *Revue d'histoire ecclésiastique*, I (1900), 41–60, 249–266, 430–477. Also Hefele-Leclercq, *Histoire des conciles*, III, 827 ff.

rejoiced still more in the Lord, who has deigned so to endow you with His grace that you have softened the hearts of that stubborn race, until they bowed with willing minds in obedient faith and yielded to the divine commands.

You inform us how deeply God has touched the hearts of our most noble sons Pippin and Karlmann so that they strive to be associates and helpers in your mission by divine inspiration. Abundant reward awaits them in heaven; for blessed is the man through whom God is blessed.

With regard to the metropolitan bishops whom you have placed in each provincial metropolis, Grimo [of Rouen], about whom we are already informed, Abel [of Rheims], and Hartbert [of Sens], we confirm them upon your recommendation and are sending them the pallium for the complete establishment [of their metropolitan rights] and for the increase of the Church of God, that they may go on to a still stronger position. As to the use of the pallium and how those who are thus privileged must show their fidelity [to the Roman See], we have sent them instructions so that they may understand when to use the pallium and how to preach to their subjects the way of salvation, that discipline, uncorrupted and unbroken, may be maintained in their churches, and that the priestly office lodged in them shall not be polluted as it was formerly, but shall be pure and acceptable unto God in so far as human conditions will allow. Let none wander away from the sacred canons, but let their offerings be pure, so that God will be pleased with their gifts and that God's people, with hearts purified from all corruption, will give evidence of the sanctifying power of the Christian religion.

You report to us, dear brother, that you have discovered in that same province of the Franks two pseudo-prophets, whom we should call not pseudo-prophets but pseudo-Christians. One of them we have found to be a new Simon according to the tenor of your letters. He even claimed to be a priest but did not in the least refrain from carnal lusts, leading people astray and preaching foolishness, not merely giving over his own soul into the power of the devil, but plunging the souls of the people into the abyss and seducing them with falsehoods, drawing them away from the

Church of God and setting them against the divine law. He set up crosses and oratories in the fields and seduced the people to desert the public churches and flock to him, deceived by false miracles which he there performed. He claimed the title of "Your Holiness," consecrated churches in his own name, and declared that he knew the names of the angels, as you described in your letter; but we declare that they are names, not of angels but rather of demons.

The other man, you say, was so given over to lust that he kept a concubine and had two children by her. And yet he clung to his priesthood, declaring that it was right, according to the Old Testament tradition, that a surviving brother should take his brother's widow to wife; also that when Christ came up from hell, he left no one there, but brought them all with him. All these things we declare to be abominable and sinful, and Your Fraternity has done well to convict the men and put them in custody and to call them the servants and forerunners of Antichrist. Fight on, then, beloved; act with energy and continue watchful in the service of Christ, that His flock may increase more and more and that you may receive abundant and eternal reward and may become, as we believe, partaker and companion of the Apostles with the chosen saints of God.

God keep you safe, most reverend brother.

Given on the tenth day before the Kalends of July, in the third year of our most pious and august Lord, Artavasdos, by God crowned emperor, in the third year of his consulship and the third year of Nicephorus emperor, in the tenth indiction.

XLVI [58]. *Pope Zacharias answers a request of Boniface to send the pallium to Grimo of Rouen alone and denies the accusation of simony* Nov. 5, 744

Zacharias, servant of the servants of God, to his very reverend and holy brother and fellow bishop, Boniface.

Upon receiving your letter, most holy brother, from the hands of the present messenger and reading it through we were greatly surprised and considerably disturbed at finding it so contradictory to your communication of last August. In that earlier letter you

informed us that a council had been held with the aid of God and
the consent and intervention of Karlmann and that you had sus-
pended from their sacred functions certain false priests as unworthy
of their office and had ordained three metropolitan archbishops,
namely: Grimo in the city called Rouen, Abel in the city called
Rheims, and Hartbert in the city called Sens. The last-named came
to us bringing your letter and also others from Pippin and Karlmann, suggesting that we should send palliums to the three metropolitans aforesaid, and this we did for the unifying and the
reformation of the churches of Christ. Now, however, upon receipt
of your new letter we were greatly amazed that whereas previously you, in common with the aforesaid princes, had proposed
three palliums you now suggest one for Grimo alone. Will Your
Fraternity inform us why you wrote first for three and afterward
for one, so that we may be clear and no longer in doubt about the
matter? [1]

We find also in your aforesaid very disturbing letter certain references to us, implying that we are violators of the canons and are
trying to nullify the tradition of the fathers and to this end have
fallen—which God forbid!—into the heresy of simony, together
with our clergy, by accepting gifts from those to whom we send
the pallium and even compelling them to make payment in money.
But, dearest brother, we pray Your Holiness never in future to
write anything of the sort, for we take it as a grievous insult to
be charged with an offense which we especially detest. Far be it
from us and from our clergy that we should sell for a price the
gift which we have received by the grace of the Holy Spirit.
In granting those three palliums at your suggestion we looked

[1] The motive of Boniface in changing his plan for the permanent organization of the Frankish Church is not clear. We have not his letters proposing the
change, and it is not until we come to No. LXX, written several years later, that
we find any explanation. There Boniface refers to No. XLVI and seems to base
his change upon the procrastinations of the princes who had made him certain
promises, unfulfilled at the date of No. LXX. The close juxtaposition of the para-
graph concerning Boniface's alleged charges of simony against the pope suggests
the possibility of an additional motive. It is possible that Grimo was the only one
of the three candidates who was free from suspicion on this account and that
Boniface suspected some kind of collusion between papal officials and Frankish
dignitaries by which the candidates were to profit.

for no advantage to ourselves. Furthermore, the letters of confirmation and instruction, which were issued from our chancery according to custom, were drawn at our own expense without any return. God forbid that the crime of simony should be charged against us by you, my brother: for all those who sell the gift of the Holy Spirit for money are anathema to us.

You have informed us also in another letter that you found in Bavaria a false priest who asserted that he was ordained bishop by us. You did well, my brother, not to trust him, since a deceitful person is deceitful in everything, and, having found him such, to suspend him from his priestly office. For we charge you on the authority of the blessed Peter, prince of the Apostles, that whomever you may find departing from the sacred canons you shall by no means suffer to debase the sacred ministry.

You desire to know whether you are to have the right of preaching in Bavaria which was granted you by our predecessor. We reply that we will not diminish but rather increase the rights bestowed upon you by our predecessor. So long as divine majesty shall permit you to live, carry on as our representative not only in Bavaria but in the whole province of Gaul the preaching mission with which you are charged, and if you discover anything contrary to the Christian religion or the provisions of the canons, strive to reform such errors according to the law of justice.

May God preserve you in safety, most reverend and holy brother.

Given on the Nones of November, in the third year of the most pious and august Lord Artavasdos, crowned by God emperor, in the third year of his consulship and the third year of Nicephorus, his son, in the thirteenth indiction.

XLVII [59]. *Acts of the Roman Synod of Oct. 25, 745. Condemnation of Aldebert and Clemens at the suggestion of Boniface*

In the name of our Lord Jesus Christ.

In the reign of the merciful and august lord, the emperor Constantine, in the twenty-sixth year of his reign and the fifth of his consulship, on the twenty-fifth day of October and the fourteenth indiction, in the Lateran Palace and the basilica of Theodorus, under the presidency of the most holy and blessed lord, Pope Zacharias, attended by the holy bishops, Epiphanius of Silva Candida, Benedict of Nomentum, Venantius of Palestrina, Gregory of Porto, Nicetas of Gabii, Theodore of Ostia, and Gratiosus of Velletri, the venerable priests, John the archpriest, Gregory, Stephen, another Stephen, Dominic, Theodore, Anastasius, George, Sergius, Jordanes, Leo, another Leo, Gregory, Stephen, Eustathius, Procopius, and Theophanius.

After the Holy Gospels had been placed in the center, in the presence of the deacons and of the whole body of the clergy, Gregory, the regional notary and nomenclator, spoke: "The pious priest Denehard, messenger of the most holy Boniface, archbishop of the province of Germany, accredited to Your Apostolic Holiness, stands without and begs to be admitted. What are your commands?" The order was given: "Let him enter." And when he had come in Zacharias, most holy and blessed pope of the Holy Catholic and Apostolic Church of the city of Rome spoke: "You brought us some time ago letters of our most reverend and holy brother, Archbishop Boniface, in which he made suggestions as to what he thought best to be done. Why, then, have you again demanded entrance into our session?"

Then Denehard, the pious priest, answered: "My Lord, when in obedience to the apostolic orders, my master Bishop Boniface, servant of Your Holiness, had called a synod in the province of the Franks and had discovered there false priests, heretics, and schismatics, namely Aldebert and Clemens, he deprived them of their priestly functions and, with the approval of the Frankish princes, caused them to be held in custody. They, however, are not doing penance according to their sentence but, on the contrary, are still leading people astray. Wherefore I am sent to present to Your Apostolic Holiness this letter of my master which I hold in my hand, that you may cause it to be read before this sacred council." The reply was: "Let the letter be received and read in our presence." Then Theophanius, regional notary and purser, received the letter and read it aloud, as follows:

To Pope Zacharias, our most exalted father and apostolic pontiff, endowed with power to rule by authority of St. Peter, prince of the Apostles, Boniface, a humble servant of the servants of God, sends greeting in the love of Christ.

Ever since, some thirty years ago, I dedicated myself to the service of the Apostolic See with the approval and at the command of the apostolic lord, Gregory [the Second], I have been accustomed to refer to the apostolic pontiff all my experiences of joy or sorrow, so that in joy we might praise God together and in sorrow I might be strengthened by his counsel. So may I now be permitted to do with you. I beseech Your Holiness as it is written: "Ask thy father, and he will show thee; thy elders, and they will tell thee!"

Be it known to you, my father, that after you had ordered my unworthy self to preside at a conference of priests and a synod in the province of the Franks, as they themselves also requested, I suffered many insults and persecutions, especially from false priests, adulterous presbyters or deacons, and carnal-minded clerks.

My chief trouble was with two well-known heretics of the worst sort, blasphemers against God and the catholic faith. One, called Aldebert, is a Gaul by birth, the other, called Clemens, is a Scot. They differ in the form of their errors, but are equal in the burden of their sins. Against these I beg your apostolic authority to protect and help my weakness and by means of your written words to lead back into the right path the people of the Franks and Gauls, so that they may no longer follow after the fables and false miracles and prophecies of the precursor of Antichrist but may be turned back to the law of the Church and the way of true doctrine. May those two heretics be consigned to prison by a word from you, if that seems right to you after I have explained to you their doctrine and their way of life. Permit no one to talk with them or have communion with them, lest any become leavened with the leaven of their teaching and so perish, but let them live in segregation according to the word of the Apostle: "Such ones are delivered unto Satan, for the destruction of the flesh, that the spirit may be saved, in the day of the Lord." And according to the Gospel precept: "If he neglect to hear the Church, let him be unto thee as a heathen man and a publican," until they learn not to blaspheme nor to divide the garment of Christ. For through them I suffer persecution and the enmity and cursing of many peoples and the Church of Christ is obstructed in its true faith and doctrine.

As regards Aldebert, they say that I have taken from them a most holy apostle and robbed them of a patron and intercessor, a doer of righteousness and a worker of miracles. But let Your Holiness hear the story of his life and judge by the fruits whether he be a ravening wolf in sheep's clothing or not. In early life he was a swindler, declaring that an angel of the Lord in human form had brought to him from the ends of the earth relics of marvelous but uncertain holiness, by which he could obtain from God whatsoever he might wish. By this deception he, as the Apostle Paul said, "crept into many houses and led captive silly women laden with sins, led away by divers lusts"—also a multitude of simple folk who said that he was a man of apostolic sanctity and had performed many signs and wonders. Then he bribed unlearned bishops, who ordained him against all the rules of the canons. Finally he rose to such audacity that he declared himself equal with the Apostles of Christ. He scorned to dedicate a church in honor of any one of the Apostles or martyrs and asked why men should desire to visit the shrines of the holy Apostles. Later he dedicated—or rather defiled—oratories to himself. He set crosses and small oratories in the fields or at springs or wherever he pleased and ordered public prayers to be said there until multitudes of people, scorning other bishops and deserting the established churches, held their celebrations in such places saying: "The merits of Saint Aldebert will help us." He distributed his own fingernails and hairs from his head to be honored [as sacred objects] and carried about with the relics of St. Peter, prince of the Apostles. Then, finally, he committed the most heinous sin and blasphemy against God. When people came and threw themselves at his feet asking to confess their sins he said to them: "I know all your hidden sins, for your secret thoughts are known to me. There is no need of confession; your past sins are forgiven you. Go back to your homes absolved in peace and safety." Everything which the Holy Gospel declares is done by hypocrites he imitated in his dress, his manner of walking, and his conduct.

The other heretic, whose name is Clemens, argues against the Catholic Church, denies and contradicts the canons of the churches of Christ, and rejects the writings and the teachings of the holy fathers, Jerome, Augustine, and Gregory. Despising the decrees of the councils, he declares according to his own interpretation that he has a right to be a bishop under Christian law even though he had two children born in adultery after he had been called by that title. Reviving the Jewish law, he maintains that it is right for a Christian, if he so please, to marry

his brother's widow. Contrary to the teaching of the holy fathers he
contends that Christ, descending to the lower world, set free all who
were imprisoned there, believers and unbelievers, those who praised God
and the worshipers of idols. And many other horrible things concerning God's predestination he sets forth contrary to the catholic faith.
Wherefore I beg you to send your written order to Duke Karlmann
that this heretic also may be put in custody, so that he may no longer
spread abroad the seed of Satan, lest perchance the whole flock be con-
taminated by one unsound sheep.

We pray that Your Holiness may enjoy health and prosperity through
length of days.

When this letter had been read the holy and blessed Pope Zacharias spoke: "You have heard, beloved brethren, what has been
read in this letter concerning those blasphemers who to their own
condemnation have been proclaiming themselves to the people as
apostles."

The holy bishops and venerable priests replied: "We have indeed heard it all, not as of apostles, but servants of Satan and
forerunners of Antichrist. For what apostle or saint ever handed
out his own hairs or fingernails to the people for relics, as this
sacrilegious and pernicious Aldebert has tried to do? Let this
wickedness be rooted out by your holy apostolic action, not only
in his case, but also in that of the sinner, Clemens, who flouts the
sacred canons and rejects the expositions of the holy fathers, Am-
brose, Augustine, and Gregory. Let them receive a sentence worthy
of their evil deeds."

Then the holy and blessed Pope Zacharias spoke: "The hour is
late today. At the next session, when we have listened to the story
of his life and the form of prayer to himself which he has composed and other practices of his, then by common consent and
with God's help we shall consider what course to take."

[THE SECOND SESSION]

[Introduction same as in First Session.]

After the Holy Gospels had been placed in the center, in the
presence of the deacons and the whole body of the clergy, Gregory,

the regional notary and nomenclator, spoke: "In accordance with
the order of Your Apostolic Holiness, given at the former session,
the pious presbyter Denehard stands without. What are your commands?" The order was given: "Let him enter." When he had
entered, the most holy and blessed Pope Zacharias spoke: "The
acts of that infamous Aldebert—and other writings of his which
you had in hand at the previous session—you will now offer to be
read in this conference."

Then Theophanius, regional notary and purser, read aloud the
man's life history, beginning as follows:

In the name of Our Lord Jesus Christ:

Here begins the life of Bishop Aldebert, holy and blessed servant of
God, illustrious and wholly fair, born a saint by the will of God. Born
of humble parents, he was crowned by the grace of God, for while he
lay in his mother's womb the grace of God came upon him, and before
his blessed nativity his mother saw as in a vision a calf emerging from
her right side. Now the calf indicated that grace which he had received
from an angel before he issued forth from the womb. . . .

When this document had been read through to the end, the
holy and blessed Pope Zacharias said: "Holy fathers, what is your
answer to these blasphemies?" Epiphanius, holy bishop of Silva
Candida, said: "Of a truth, Apostolic Lord, the heart of Your
Apostolic Holiness was moved by divine inspiration when you
commissioned our aforesaid holy brother, Bishop Boniface, acting
with the chiefs of the Franks, to bring together in that region after
a long interval a council of priests, that these schisms and blasphemies might no longer be hidden from Your Apostolic Holiness."

The holy and blessed Pope Zacharias said: "If the pious priest
Denehard has anything further to bring before us let him bring it."
Denehard, the pious priest, said: "I have here a letter used by
Aldebert, which he declared was from Jesus and had fallen from
heaven." Theophanius read it aloud as follows:

In the name of God: Here begins the letter of Our Lord Jesus
Christ the son of God, which fell down in Jerusalem and was found
by the Archangel Michael near the gate Effrem. The very same copy
was read by a priest named Icore, who sent the same letter to another

priest named Talasius in the city Geremia. This Talasius sent the same
letter to another priest named Leoban in the city Arabia. The same
Leoban sent the letter to the city Uetfania, and Macrius, a priest of
God, received that letter and sent the same to Mont St. Michel. And
the same letter came by the hand of the angel of God to the city of
Rome, to the tomb of St. Peter where the keys of the kingdom of
heaven are kept. And twelve ecclesiastical dignitaries who are in the
city of Rome held vigils with fasting and prayer for three days and
nights. . . .

And so on the document was read to the end.

The holy and blessed Pope Zacharias spoke: "Of a truth, beloved
brethren, this Aldebert is mad, and all who make use of this
wickedly invented letter are lacking in mind and memory like
children or senseless women. But, that he may no longer mislead
the simple, we cannot leave the matter without discussion and a
judgment against him."

The holy bishops and the venerable priests replied: "We perceive that the heart of Your Apostolic Holiness is enlightened
with light from God and your utterances proceed from the Holy
Spirit. Wherefore let sentence be pronounced against both these
men as you shall determine."

The holy and blessed Pope Zacharias spoke: "Not as determined
by us alone but in common with Your Holinesses the matter is
to be fully considered. If it please God, when all the documents
shall have been read, sentence shall be rendered at the next
session, justly and as God shall dictate to his servants."

[THE THIRD SESSION]

[Introduction same as in the two previous sessions.]

After the Holy Gospels had been placed in the center, in the
presence of the deacons and the whole body of the clergy, Gregory,
the regional notary and nomenclator, spoke: "In accordance with
the order of Your Apostolic Holiness in the former session that the
pious presbyter Denehard should present himself before you today, he stands without. What are your commands?" The order
was given: "Let him enter." And when he had come in, the most

holy and blessed Pope Zacharias said: "Have you any further writings of those sacrilegious men to present for reading before the
synod?" The pious presbyter Denehard answered: "I have also,
my Lord, here in my hand a prayer to himself which Aldebert
tried to put together. Will you order it to be received?"

[Theophanius] took it and read it, beginning as follows:

O Lord God Almighty, Father of our Lord Jesus Christ, the Son
of God, Alpha and Omega, who sittest upon the seventh throne above
the cherubim and seraphim, great mercy and abundant sweetness are
with Thee. Father of the holy angels, maker of heaven and earth, the
sea and all that in them is, I call and cry aloud and summon Thee to
wretched me, because Thou hast deigned to promise: "Whatsoever
thou shalt ask of the Father in my name shall be given thee." To Thee
I pray, to Thee I cry aloud, to Christ the Lord I commit my soul.

And as he read in order, he came to the place where he said:

I pray and conjure and beseech ye, Angel Uriel, Angel Raguel, Angel
Tubuel, Angel Michael, Angel Adinus, Angel Tubuas, Angel Sabaoc,
and Angel Simiel.

When this sacrilegious prayer had been read through, the
most holy and blessed Pope Zacharias said: "Holy brethren, what
is your answer?" The most holy bishops and venerable priests
replied: "What else can be done but to burn with fire all that
has been read to us and punish the authors with the bonds of
anathema? The eight names of angels which Aldebert calls upon
in his prayer are not names of angels, except Michael, but rather
of demons whom he has summoned to his aid. We, instructed by
Your Apostolic Holiness and by divine authority, know the names
of but three angels: Michael, Gabriel, and Raphael, whereas he
brought in the names of demons under the disguise of angels."
The holy and blessed Pope Zacharias said: "Your Holinesses have
decided wisely that all his writings deserve to be burned with fire;
but, as a means of confuting them, it will be well to preserve
them in our sacred archives for his perpetual condemnation. And
now that all the evidence is at hand we will proceed to pass sentence
upon the two men mentioned above."

The Council unanimously voted:

"Whereas Aldebert, whose acts and infamous opinions have been read to us, saw fit to call himself an apostle and to distribute his own hairs and fingernails to the people as relics, leading them astray with various errors and summoning demons to his aid under the guise of angels, let him be deprived of all priestly functions, doing penance for his sins, and let him no longer seduce the people. But, if he shall persist in his errors and continue to mislead the people let him be anathema and be condemned by the eternal judgment of God—him and all who share his opinions or follow his teachings, or become associated with him.

"And Clemens also, who in his folly rejects the statutes of the holy fathers and all decrees of councils, imposing Judaism upon Christians and preaching marriage with a brother's widow, saying also that our Lord Jesus Christ, after he had descended into the lower world, brought everyone thence, righteous and unrighteous—let him also be stripped of his priestly functions, bound with the chains of anathema, and condemned by the judgment of God; likewise all who shall assent to his sacrilegious teachings."

ZACHARIAS, bishop of the Holy, Catholic, and Apostolic Church of God of the city of Rome, affixed his signature to the acts and the sentences promulgated by us.

EPIPHANIUS, bishop of the Holy Church of Silva Candida

BENEDICT, bishop of the Holy Church of Nomentum

VENANTIUS, bishop of the Holy Church of Palestrina

GREGORY, bishop of the Holy Church of Porto

NICETAS, bishop of the Holy Church of Gabii

THEODORE, bishop of the Holy Church of Ostia

GRATIOSUS, bishop of the Holy Church of Velletri

JOHN, archpriest of the title of Saint Susanna

GREGORY, humble priest of the Holy Roman Church of the title of St. Clement

STEPHEN, by the grace of God priest of the Holy Roman Church of the title of St. Mark

STEPHEN, unworthy priest of the Holy Roman Church of the title of St. Eusebius

DOMINIC, humble priest of the Holy Roman Church of the title of St. Prisca

THEODORE, humble priest of the Holy Roman Church of the title of St. Lawrence

ANASTASIUS, unworthy priest of the Holy Roman Church of the title of St. Mary

GEORGE, humble priest of the Holy Roman Church of the title of Saints John and Paul

SERGIUS, humble priest of the Holy Roman Church of the title of St. Potentiana

JORDANES, unworthy priest of the Holy Roman Church of the title of St. Sabina

THEOPHANIUS, humble priest of the Holy Roman Church of the title of the *Quatuor Coronati*

LEO, unworthy priest of the Holy Roman Church of the title of St. Anastasia

LEO, humble priest of the Holy Roman Church of the title of St. Damasus

GREGORY, unworthy priest of the Holy Roman Church of the title of St. Balbina

STEPHEN, priest of the Holy Roman Church of the title of St. Chrysogonus

EUSTATHIUS, humble priest of the Holy Roman Church

PROCOPIUS, unworthy priest of the Holy Roman Church of the title of St. Cyriacus

XLVIII [60]. *Pope Zacharias to Boniface regarding the Frankish synods; he approves the establishment of an archbishopric at Cologne; church reforms*   Oct. 31, 745

Zacharias, servant of the servants of God, to his very reverend and holy brother and fellow bishop, Boniface.

When your letter, most holy brother, was brought to us and we had caused it to be read in detail, we learned from the whole series of your letters that, for our sins, while you were striving to sow the seeds of the Lord's grain for the increase of the spiritual harvest, suddenly enemies began to sow tares with them and so to hinder your good work. But now do you and your brethren be instant in prayer; build yourselves tools of the spirit, root out the weeds and burn them. As the blessed Gregory says: "Let your will persist in doing the good work, and God will bring it to fulfillment." And so, my dearest brother, take comfort in the Lord thy helper.

As to the raiding of the heathen against your people, it grieves us sorely; but let not this adversity disturb you. The city of Rome was often ravaged for its iniquities and yet God deigned to restore it by His almighty power. And so, we believe, he will comfort you. But, reverend brother, urge the peoples entrusted to you to fast and to offer supplications and litanies, to the God of all grace, and his abundant mercy shall come to your aid. Let no adversity distress you, we repeat, but press on in the good work you have begun. And we, unworthy sinner that we are, will assist you as far as we are able with our own prayers and those of our colleagues.

In regard to the synod held in the territory of the Franks through the mediation of our most noble sons Pippin and Karlmann, in accordance with our written directions and under the leadership of Your Holiness acting in our stead, we know what you have accomplished and give thanks to Almighty God who has strengthened their hearts to aid you in this pious work. You have carried it all through admirably and in accordance with the canons, as well in the case of the false, corrupt, and schismatic bishops, as also of those others, priests in name only, who were acting contrary to the canons or against the Catholic and Apostolic Church of God. On these points we reply according to the several items of your report.

We have received with joyful heart, as done by God's will, the news that the Frankish princes have chosen a city in those parts of Germany where you formerly preached, up to the border of the lands of the heathen, that you may have there for all time a metropolitan see from which you may guide other bishops in the way of righteousness and of which your successors may have legal possession in perpetuity. And although false and schismatic priests have striven to prevent this, the Lord will scatter their futile efforts and will establish what is in accordance with the decrees of the fathers. Those princes of the Franks who have aided you in this undertaking will receive from Almighty God full reward and unnumbered blessings.

Likewise, in the case of that false bishop whom you have described as the son of an adulterate and homicidal clerk, born in adultery and brought up without discipline, and who, among other horrible things, has ordained priests like unto himself—you remember, reverend brother, that we have more than once written to you that no murderer or adulterer or fornicator may be allowed to degrade the sacred ministry, neither men undergoing penance nor any to whom the sacred canons forbid ordination. On the other hand, Your Fraternity will investigate in regard to persons baptized and churches consecrated by them, and if it shall appear that they consecrated churches or baptized infants in the name of the Trinity during their priesthood, let the consecration of churches and the baptism of children be confirmed.

You have indicated that priests whom you had rejected have been absolved by us and are now scattered about the territory of the Franks. Do not believe this for a moment, my brother. If we had done so—which is impossible—we should have informed Your Affection by letter. Never believe the impossible. We do not preach one thing and do or order another, as those babblers say, but with God's help we follow to the end what we teach. And we exhort Your Holiness to stand fast by the ordinances of the holy fathers, as we also in no way teach or act otherwise.

In regard to your petition that we would write to the princes and to others of the Franks: we have sent word to them severally that they are to be friendly to you and are to assist you in the Lord's work.

In the matter of land rentals, you were not able to obtain from the Franks their full restitution to churches and monasteries, but only that each family of serfs shall pay at the end of the year twelve *denarii*. Thanks be to God that you could get this much, and when God shall grant us peace, then offerings for the saints will increase in place of those which are now, as you inform us, cut off by the pressure of Saracens, Saxons, and Frisians.

You inquire about the case of priests deposed from their office on account of serious crimes, whom you have found guilty of adultery or murder, so that they cannot be either priests or clerks and are not willing to do penance as monks, but go to the king's palace and beg him to grant them lands of churches or monasteries where they may lead a secular life and squander the property of the saints. On this point also we have advised the Frankish princes what action they are to take.

In your second letter we find an account of all that those false and schismatic bishops, Aldebert and Clemens, have done in opposition to you, with details as to their acts and their impious errors. This report of the infamous actions of these scoundrels we caused to be read in presence of our assembled brethren and colleagues; and when it had been read before the council, they all cried out with one voice in fervent zeal that their doctrines as well as that infamous biography of himself which Aldebert caused to be written ought to be burnt with fire. But we decided that it would be better not to do this, and gave orders to have them kept forever in the archives of our Holy Church for the conviction of their authors, who also have received their well-deserved sentence. A duplicate of this document has been sent to Your Holiness, so that when it has been read in Frankland every schismatic who hears this judgment of the Holy Catholic and Apostolic Church of God may be converted from his evil ways.

In your third letter you inform us about another false teacher named Gewilip [of Mainz] who formerly held unlawfully the office of bishop and who, you say, is now hurrying to Rome without the sanction of anyone. When he arrives, such action shall be taken as may please God.

It is our wish that Your Reverence, having made a beginning with God's help, shall continue every year at a convenient season to hold a council in the country of the Franks, so that by means of the assembled priests and the ordinances of the sacred canons no dangers may be able to develop, but rather the unity of the Church of God and the catholic and apostolic discipline may be spread everywhere in those parts and the whole people, even in the extreme West, may be truly catholic and may no longer be involved in the errors of false priests and so be plunged into destruction. When you assemble a council, come to such an agreement with the metropolitans whom we have confirmed, on the point you have made, that no member shall be received without letters of recommendation. In regard to this and all other questions we have sent letters of advice to the Frankish princes, as we have already said.

The city formerly called Agrippina, but now named Cologne, at the request of the Franks and by a decision of our authority, we have confirmed as a metropolis assigned to you and we have sent to Your Holiness the charter of institution of this metropolitan church for all time.

May God keep you in safety, most reverend and holy brother.

Given on the eve of the Kalends of November, in the twenty-seventh year of our most pious and august Lord Constantine, by God crowned emperor, in the fifth year of his consulship, in the fourteenth indiction.

XLIX [61]. *Pope Zacharias urges the Frankish clergy and laity to support the reforms of Boniface*   [Oct., 745]

Pope Zacharias to all bishops, priests, deacons, and abbots, all dukes and counts, and all God-fearing men throughout Gallia and the provinces of the Franks.[1]

Upon the report of our most reverend and holy brother, Bishop Boniface, that he had brought together a synod in your country according to our directions and with the concurrence of our sons your princes Pippin and Karlmann, he himself presiding in our stead, and that the Lord had inclined your hearts, together with those of your princes, to obey his instructions, and that you had cast out false, schismatic, murderous, and unchaste priests, we returned thanks to our God Omnipotent and prayed without ceasing that he who has begun this good work among you may continue it to the end.

[1] During the seventh and eighth centuries the term "France" had not yet acquired a fixed geographical meaning. Chroniclers and hagiographers as well as public documents used it now for Neustria alone and now, in a broader sense, to include other regions also. (Leclercq, *Dictionnaire de liturgie et d'archéologie chrétienne*, Vol. V, col. 2123 ff.) The Roman Curia in this letter uses the old term "Gallia" meaning perhaps the southern part of the country and then the indefinite phrase "Francorum provincias" for the rest of the Frankish domains, including those in Germany.

I beseech you all before God steadfastly to follow his instructions. We have appointed him in our stead to preach in those parts, that with God's help he may guide you into the right way and that you may be saved from all evil-doing. For up till now you have, for your sins, had false and misleading priests. Wherefore all the heathen peoples prevailed over you in fight, since you made no distinction between laymen and priests for whom fighting is unlawful. For what kind of a victory can there be when priests who at one moment are performing the sacred mysteries and offering the body of the Lord Christ, in the next are slaughtering with sacrilegious hands Christians, to whom they ought to be administering the sacraments, or pagans, to whom they ought to be preaching Christ? The word of God says: "Ye are the salt of the earth; but if the salt have lost its savor, wherewith shall it be salted? It is henceforth good for nothing but to be cast out and trodden under foot of men."

This being so, if you have such priests among you, how can you be victorious over your enemies? But if your priests are pure and clean of all unchastity and blood-guiltiness, as the sacred canons teach and as our brother Boniface preaches in our stead, and if you are in all things obedient to him, no people can stand before you, but all pagans shall fall before your face and you shall remain victors. And more, for your well-doing you shall inherit eternal life.

And you, beloved brethren, who are true priests or who are living under regular discipline, show yourselves to be truly ministers of God and dispensers of his mysteries, so that his ministry be not blamed and the saying, "Like people, like priest," be not true of you. If that were so, how could you expect the praise of men or the recompense of God? But so govern yourselves that you may be true priests and may bring such others into the priesthood that both you and they may have good witness among those who are without. And so may you gain the praise of men and win from God the reward of eternal happiness, because through you those who have blameless priests have been led into the true faith of Christ. Come together every year to take counsel for the unity of the Church, and whatever may be contrary to this, root it out, that the Church of God may remain unshaken.

Farewell.

L [62]. *The Roman Cardinal-Deacon Gemmulus sends Boniface an account of the Roman synod of 745* [745]

To our most holy master, Archbishop Boniface, endowed with apostolic virtues, Gemmulus, an unworthy deacon of the Holy Apostolic See.

I have received your revered and God-pleasing letter and read it with all due respect and great veneration. And because after so long a time I was found worthy to receive a word from you, I gave thanks to Almighty God, who has cheered me, his unworthy servant, with the news of your well-being. All the directions which you give us in this letter we have carried out as God has been pleased to permit. Those suggestions also which you have made to our Apostolic Lord were received by us, reported, and read to him, who entrusted the matter to us. Please understand that all the documents sent by him to you were drawn up and put in form by us according to your wishes.

Also we made a suggestion which you had not expected. A synod of the clergy was held, our Apostolic Lord presiding. The scandalous life of the wretch Aldebert was reviewed and all his works were laid before the synod together with the letter of Your Paternal Holiness in which you refer to him and to the insanities of Clemens. Thereupon a sentence of anathema was pronounced against them and all who belonged to their accursed sect, and a copy of this was forwarded to you by our Apostolic Lord. All this was done in the presence of our brother, the reverend priest Denehard, who can assure you by word of mouth that it was done through us.

Pray understand, most holy father, that I stand ready to comply with your directions in every respect, asking only that you will order prayers in my behalf. For I know that I have been snatched from the temptations of the enemy by the aid of your prayers and that a merciful God has bestowed healing upon his servant. Hemmed in by diverse frailties, I follow unworthily that word of the Apostle: "When I am weak, then am I strong," and also: "Most gladly, therefore, will I rather glory in my infirmities, that the strength of Christ may rest upon me," through your holy prayers.

Our reverend sisters and handmaids of God who came to the threshold of the holy princes of the Apostles with introductions to us from you, we have cared for as God has deigned to give us strength, for the sake of your sacred recommendation. We have received also the gift which you sent us—a silver cup and a piece of cloth, a gift doubly precious to us as coming from so honored a father. Though we cannot repay you in kind, still we send in exchange of loving remembrance four ounces of cinnamon, four ounces of costmary, two pounds of pepper, and one pound of *cozumber*.

I beg you to accept these without offense, and I implore you by all means to offer prayers for us.

May divine majesty keep Your Holy Paternity in safety and in prayer for us, our father and master, endowed with apostolic merits.

LI [63]. *Boniface to Bishop Daniel of Winchester, describing the obstacles to his work and asking for a manuscript of the Prophets*   [742–746]

To his beloved master, Bishop Daniel, Boniface, servant of the servants of God, sends sincere and affectionate greeting.

It is a well-known custom among men when anything sad or burdensome happens to them, to seek for comfort and advice from those in whose friendship and wisdom they have especial confidence. And so I, trusting to your well-proven fatherly wisdom and friendship, am laying before you the troubles of my weary mind and am asking your advice and comfort. We have not only, as the Apostle says, "fightings without and fears within," but we have fightings within as well as fears, caused especially by false priests and hypocrites, enemies of God, ruining themselves, misleading the people with scandals and false doctrines, and crying to them, as the prophet says, "Peace! Peace! when there is no peace." They strive to cover and choke with weeds or to turn into poisonous grain the seed of the Word which we have received from the bosom of the Catholic and Apostolic Church and have tried to sow. What we plant they do not water that it may increase but try to uproot that it may wither away, offering to the people and teaching them new divisions and errors of divers sorts. Some abstain from foods which God made for our use; some nourish themselves only with milk and honey, rejecting all other foods; some declare— and this is most harmful to the people—that murderers or adulterers who persist in their crimes may nevertheless be priests of God. But the people, as the Apostle says, "will not endure sound doctrine but after their own lusts shall heap to themselves teachers."

Now we, needing the patronage of the Frankish court, cannot separate ourselves from contact with such persons, as the canonical rule requires—excepting only that in the holy ceremony of the Mass we do not communicate with them in the sacred mystery of the body and blood of the Lord. We avoid taking counsel with them or obtaining their consent; for to such men our labors with the heathen and with the mixed multitude of common people seem wholly foreign. But when someone from our ranks, priest, deacon, clerk, or monk, leaves the bosom of Mother Church and departs from the true faith, then he breaks out with the pagans into abuse of the sons of the Church. This is a terrible obstacle to the Gospel of the glory of Christ.

In all these matters we seek first your intercession with God that we may finish the course of our ministry without injury to our soul. We pray you from the depths of our heart to intercede for us, that God, the gracious comforter of his laborers, may keep our souls safe and free from sin in the midst of such tempestuous times.

As to holding communion with the priests above mentioned I am very anxious to hear and to follow your wholesome counsel. Without the support of the Frankish prince I can neither govern the members of the Church nor defend the priests, clerks, monks, and maids of God; nor can I, without orders from him and the fear inspired by him, prevent the pagan rites and the sacrilegious worship of idols in Germany. But when I go to him to secure his aid in these matters I cannot possibly avoid personal contact with men of that sort, as the canon law requires; I can only refuse agreement with them. I fear the guilt of such communication, remembering that at the time of my ordination, by the command of Pope Gregory, I swore by the body of St. Peter to refuse communion with men of that kind, unless I could convert them to the way of the Church law. But I fear still more the injury to the preaching which I am bound to give to the people, if I am unable to go to the prince of the Franks. Pray let me know what you, my Father, may see fit to decide, to adjudge, and to command for your disturbed and hesitating son. For my part, I feel that I am sufficiently segregated from them if I refrain from taking counsel with them, from seeking their consent, and from joining with them in church services, when they are not in good canonical standing.

There is one solace in my mission I should like, if I may be so bold, to ask of your fatherly kindness, namely, that you send me the book of the Prophets which Abbot Winbert of reverend memory, my former teacher, left when he passed from this life to the Lord, and in which the six Prophets are contained in one volume in clear letters written in full. If God shall incline your heart to do this, you could not give me a greater comfort in my old age nor bring yourself greater assurance of reward. I cannot procure in this country such a book of the Prophets as I need, and with my fading sight I cannot read well writing which is small and filled with abbreviations. I am asking for this book because it is copied clearly, with all letters distinctly written out.

Meanwhile, I send you by the priest Forthere a letter and a little gift as a token of my sincere affection, a bath towel, not of pure silk, but mixed with rough goat's hair, to dry your feet.

I learned recently from a priest who came directly from you to Germany that you have suffered blindness. You know better than I, my master, who said, "Whom the Lord loveth he chasteneth"; and Paul, the Apostle, says: "When I am weak, then am I strong"; and "My power is made perfect in weakness"; and the Psalmist, "Many are the afflictions of the righteous." You, my father, have, as Anthony is reputed to have said of Didymus, eyes that can see

God and His angels and the glorious raptures of the heavenly Jerusalem. Wherefore I believe, trusting in your wisdom and patience, that God has sent this trial for the perfecting of your strength and the increase of your merit and that by means of it you may see more clearly with the eyes of the spirit and may desire all the more the things which God loves and requires and may so much the less see and desire what God loves not but forbids. For what are our bodily eyes in these perilous times but, so to speak, windows of sin, through which we look upon sins or sinners or, worse still, bring sins upon our own selves by what we see and lust after?

That Your Holiness may be well and may offer prayers for me in Christ is my earnest desire.

LII [64]. *Bishop Daniel of Winchester replies to the inquiries and*
    complaints of Boniface   [742–746]

To the very reverend master, Archbishop Boniface, worthy to be honored by all men of the true faith for his varied knowledge and his many and gracious virtues, Daniel, servant of God's people, sends his sincere greetings in the Lord who is above the highest heavens.

Upon reading your letter, our brother, we were greatly troubled, for it seems unbearable to those who love when misfortune befalls those who love them. And yet, upon further reflection, we found a certain comfort in the thought that the incredible craftiness of our artful enemy would never have tried to overturn your religious work with such violence and such varied forms of attack through the high-placed persons of priests or other evil-minded men, if he had not perceived extraordinary excellence in that work. You ought, therefore, above all things to make every effort that the glorious beginning which, to my mind, is worthy of comparison with the struggles of the Apostles, shall on no account be abandoned because of the traps set by foxy men who make a practice of resisting the doctrine of salvation. Our trials are the easier to bear, the more certain we are that saints and martyrs have tribulation in this world but most abundant rewards in heaven, according to

God's promise. If only we do not weary in endurance God will be our helper here, and in the world beyond we shall be worthy of His reward, rejoicing with the righteous. Since, therefore, Your Excellence has seen fit to ask advice from our insignificance, we think you should aim to endure with infinite patience that which, as you know full well, can happen only through divine providence.

Certainly outward conflicts are a cruel affliction and strife within still more to be dreaded—and no wonder, for Jesus Christ bore witness that brother should deliver up brother to death, and the father his child, and parents should be slain by children for His name's sake. You say that wicked men attack and try to destroy the work of God by superstitious discriminations about food, which is equally almost totally destroyed by its consumption by man, or else that they seek dishonest gains by means of adulation; they lull the people into false security by praising them and abusing you and keep repeating with feigned sincerity the sweet word "peace," and, as the prophet Isaiah had foreseen, call "evil good and good evil." They try to choke the harvest entrusted to Your Reverence by sowing barren tares all over it. But because in a certain passage of the Scripture it is forbidden to root out the tares before the grain is ripe, and because, though those men put forward unheard-of doctrines to deceive the mind of the ignorant, such doctrines and the refutation of them are not hidden from you, who have perfect familiarity and not merely a slight acquaintance with the Scripture—because of this (not to detain you longer with details) I say briefly that in spite of all the means used by that wicked faction to annoy and defeat you, nevertheless you are to follow the example of the holy men of the past and you must endure with patience what cannot be set right by correction.

As to the priesthood of murderers and adulterers, who refuse to repent and dare to continue in their sins: the sacred canons and the decrees of pontiffs give you ample directions. If the perfecting of life—that is, the grace of the communion of Christ—is granted only before death to murderers who have repented, how can the office of ruling a Christian society be entrusted to men who are still impenitent? And the adulterer who even to the last does not repent of his shameless conduct, by what reasoning shall he usurp the priestly office? According to the decrees of Pope Innocent and others, he who marries a widow or a second wife is excluded not only from any office in the Church but even from the clergy. Although concessions have been made in these cases on account of human frailty, adultery is forbidden by all authorities.

As to communion with false brethren or priests, how practical would be the decision to keep away from them in temporal matters, while they try to force themselves in always and everywhere, unless you were ready to get out of the world altogether?

Paul the Apostle declares that he was involved in these same dangers, and other founders of the Christian religion admit that they suffered in the same way and predicted that their followers would have to suffer also.

You say that you avoid all contact with those people in the sacred liturgy, lest you seem to be casting that which is holy before the dogs, and I will explain later what St. Augustine's opinion was upon this point. You say further that you dwell among them not voluntarily, not in agreement with them nor of your own pleasure, but only occasionally as necessity requires. Jerome says: "In the Gospel good will is demanded, and even if it has no result, it will not fail of its reward." And, for the sake of argument, if you associate with them in partaking of food or in residence did not he who "came not to call the righteous," etc., go to the banquets of sinners for the purpose of teaching them? And, as to your going to the king sometimes with them to secure peace for the Church, since they pretend to be acting like true pastors for the good of their sheep, let us remember that the first thing is to fulfill what is written, "be ye subject to every ordinance of man," etc., and "to all higher powers," etc. Then we must consider that the figure of the wheat and the tares signifies the mingling of good and bad men. And Augustine says—that both clean and unclean animals entered into the ark and that the unclean did not enter through any breach in the ark but through one and the same door which the builder had made. "For," he says, "by means of these figures and declarations the good receive, not a counsel of slothfulness, so that they may be indifferent to things which they ought to prevent, but a counsel of patience to bear what they cannot change —saving always the true doctrine." He says also:

When, therefore, we find in the Church evil men whom we cannot re-form or control by the Church discipline, then let not the wicked and dangerous conceit rise up in our hearts that we ought to separate our-selves from them lest we be involved in their sins and so try to draw after us as pure and holy disciples men who are separated from the bond of unity as from the company of evildoers. Let us remember those parables of Scripture in which it is shown that the evil are to be mingled with the good in the Church even to the end of the world and the day of judgment, and that no harm can come to the good from participating with them in the sacraments, since they have not consented to their doings. But when those who govern the Church can use also, without causing great disturbance, the power of discipline over the unruly or the wicked, then certainly, lest we fall asleep in dull indifference, we must be roused by the spur of those other precepts which lay stress upon severity and compulsion.

Thus there is a time for dissimulation and for toleration of evil men within the Church and again there is a time for punishing and reform-ing them, not admitting them to communion or excluding them from it, so that we need not be slothful under the pretext of being patient, nor cruel under cover of being diligent.

I will tell you also what I have culled from the works of ancient scholars, things useful to bear in mind in the midst of such ruinous barbarism. If perchance, in the course of the above-mentioned com-promise you should be charged by some one with any sort of dis-simulation or even of deception, we read that useful deceit may at times be practiced. For example, "Cephas withdrew and separated himself, fearing them"; and Paul, the Vessel of Election, shaved his head and circumcised Timothy. Even the Son of God pretended that he was going farther and that he did not know things which he did know, as it says in the Gospel: "Who hath touched me," and: "Where have ye laid him?" The Psalmist disguised his face before Abimelech, and Joseph spoke deceitfully with his brethren. Israel also covered his loins with goat skins. He did this that he might be taken for some one else, and if it be carefully considered, it was not falsehood but a mystery. The goat skins were the symbol of sins, and he who clothed himself in them signifies the one who bears the sins of others.

We have written these things to you not as if you were ignorant of the ancient authorities or were in need of instruction from our simplicity but with great hesitation, because we were anxious not to disappoint you and because we learned that you were in difficulties with your superiors. Moved by love and a sense of duty rather than relying upon our skill or assurance, not commanding but only expounding, we have brought forward these things lest we might seem to be in any way opposed to those who are beyond measure more distinguished than ourself.

Your encouraging advice as to how to bear the heavy burden of ill health was very welcome, and as far as our strength permits and with the help of God, whose mercy counsels us, we shall follow your wholesome words.

May your kind affection be assured that although we are separated by the vast extent of land and sea and the wide diversity of climate we are afflicted by the same scourge of sorrows. The work of Satan is the same there and here. Wherefore I earnestly pray that we may fortify each other by mutual exchange of prayers, ever mindful of His word: "Where two or three are gathered together."

Farewell, farewell, my hundredfold dearest friend!

LIII [65]. *Boniface to Abbess Eadburga of Thanet* [742–746]

To his sister, the abbess Eadburga, in the bond of spiritual love and with a holy and virginal kiss of affection, Boniface, bishop and legate of the Roman Church, sends greeting in Christ.

We beseech your loving-kindness with earnest prayer to intercede for us with the Creator of all things. That you may know the reason for this request let me tell you that, for our sins, the way of our wandering is beset by tempests of many kinds. On every hand is struggle and grief, fighting without and fear within. Worst of all, the treachery of false brethren surpasses the malice of unbelieving pagans. Pray, therefore, the merciful defender of our lives, the only refuge of the afflicted, the Lamb of God who has taken away the sins of the world, to keep us safe from harm with his sheltering right hand as we go among the dens of such wolves; that where there should be the lovely feet of those who bear the torch of Gospel peace, there may not be the dark and wandering footsteps of apostates, but that when our loins are girded the Father all-merciful may put blazing torches in our hands to enlighten the hearts of the Gentiles to the vision of the Gospel of the glory of Christ.

And I pray also that you may be pleased to make intercession for those heathen who have been given into our charge by the Apostolic See, that the Savior of the world may see fit to rescue them from the worship of idols and join them to the sons of the only Catholic Mother Church to the praise and glory of His name whose will it is that all men shall be saved and shall come to the knowledge of the truth.

Farewell.[1]

LIV [68]. *Pope Zacharias to Boniface concerning cases of rebaptism in Bavaria*   July 1, 746

Zacharias, servant of the servants of God, to his very reverend and holy brother and fellow bishop, Boniface.

Virgilius and Sedonius, men leading the religious life in Bavaria, have informed us in their letters that you, reverend brother, have enjoined them to administer baptism a second time to certain Christians. This news has disturbed us not a little, and, if the facts are as reported, has greatly surprised us. They stated that there was in that province a priest who was entirely ignorant of Latin and who, in the baptismal service, not understanding the Latin idiom, made the mistake of saying: "*Baptizo te in nomine patria*

---

[1] Two letters of like import follow in Tangl's edition (Nos. 66, 67). They are here omitted.

et filia et spiritus sancti." And on this account you, reverend brother, thought a new baptism to be necessary.

But, most holy brother, if the ministrant introduced no error or heresy but simply through ignorance made a slip in the Latin language, we cannot agree that the baptism should be repeated. For, as you well know, not even one baptized by heretics in the name of the Father and the Son and the Holy Spirit is to be rebaptized, but only to be absolved by the laying on of hands. If, then, the case stands as reported to us, you are no longer to give instruction to this effect, but Your Holiness will strive to follow the teaching and preaching of the holy fathers.

May God keep you in safety, most reverend brother.

Given on the Kalends of July, the twenty-sixth year of our most pious and august Lord Constantine, emperor crowned by God, in the fourth year of his consulship, in the fourteenth indiction.

LV [69]. *Boniface to King Ethelbald of Mercia*   [745-746]

To his reverend and beloved lord, Ethelbald, king of Mercia, Boniface, servant of the servants of God, sends affectionate greetings.

We beg Your Gracious Highness to afford my messenger Ceola, bearer of this letter, your aid and protection in my affairs and in his travels and in whatever way his errand may require. May you receive your reward in God's name for the assistance you gave in every way to our messengers a year ago, as they have reported to us.

As a token of true affection and devoted friendship we are sending you a hawk and two falcons, two shields and two lances, and we beg you to accept these trifling gifts for the sake of our affection toward you. "Let us all hear the end of the discourse: Fear God and obey his commandments."

We ask also that if any writings of ours shall come to your hand by another messenger you will be pleased to give them your attention and your utmost care.

Farewell in Christ.

LVI [72]. *Ingalice, priest, to Lullus, deacon, sending him some
small gifts*   [c. 740–746]

To the honorable and much beloved Lullus, minister of God,
Ingalice, unworthy priest but your entirely devoted servant, greetings in the Lord.

Your wise letter with the gifts of your generosity, addressed to
me, has reached my hands. I read the letter with diligence and
attention and understand, if I am not wrong, that you, after having
so gracefully saluted us, humbly request us to give you, for what
it is worth, the support of our prayers against all temptations and
all hostilities and tribulations which often in this world harass the
servants of God, according to the saying of the Apostle: "All that
will live godly in Christ Jesus shall suffer persecution." Wherefore
the whole congregation here has offered continuously prayers to
God for your welfare. And now, my beloved deacon, since in an-
swering your very learned letter I cannot write anything equally
worthy because I have so little talent, let me remark that true
charity endureth everything.

With these uncouth words of mine I am sending some very
small gifts to be brought before your kind presence, four knives
made by us in our fashion, a bundle of reed pens, and one towel,
as a reminder of our love for you. I beg Your Fraternity to accept
them in the same spirit in which they are offered. The whole
group of our brothers with the abbot wish to salute, in the love of
God, our intercessor with the Lord, the venerable prelate Boniface.

LVII [73]. *A letter of advice from Boniface and other bishops to
King Ethelbald of Mercia*   [746–747]

To his dearest master, King Ethelbald, cherished in the love of
Christ above all other kings and holding glorious sway over the
realm of the Anglians, Boniface, archbishop and legate of the
Roman Church in Germany, and his fellow bishops, Wera, Burk-
hardt, Werbert, Abel, and Willibald, send greetings of unfailing
love in Christ.

We acknowledge before God and the holy angels, that when
we have heard through trustworthy messengers of your prosperity,

your faith in God, and your good works before God and man we have returned joyful thanks to God, praying and beseeching the Savior of the world to keep you forever safe and steadfast in faith and works before God and in the leadership of the people of Christ. But when we hear that any harm befalls you, be it in the conditions of your government or the event of war or, worse yet, some peril to your soul's welfare, we are afflicted with pain and sorrow; for by God's will we rejoice with you in your joy and grieve with you in your sorrow.

We have heard that you are very liberal in almsgiving, and congratulate you thereon; for they who give to the least of their needy brethren shall hear at the day of judgment, according to Gospel truth, the gracious word of the Lord: "Inasmuch as ye have done it unto the least of these my brethren, ye have done it unto me. Come, ye blessed of my Father, inherit the kingdom prepared for you from the foundation of the world." We have heard also that you repress robbery and wrongdoing, perjury, and rapine with a strong hand, that you are famed as a defender of widows and of the poor, and that you have established peace within your kingdom. In this also we have rejoiced, because the Truth itself and our Peace, which is Christ, said, "Blessed are the peacemakers, for they shall be called the children of God."

But amidst all this, one evil report as to the manner of life of Your Grace has come to our hearing, which has greatly grieved us and which we could wish were not true. We have learned from many sources that you have never taken to yourself a lawful wife. Now this relation was ordained of the Lord God himself from the very beginning of the world and was repeatedly insisted upon by the Apostle Paul saying: "On account of fornication let every man have his own wife, and every woman have her own husband." If you had willed to do this for the sake of chastity and abstinence, or had refrained from women from the fear and love of God and had given evidence that you were abstinent for God's sake we should rejoice, for that is not worthy of blame but rather of praise. But if, as many say—but which God forbid!—you have neither taken a lawful spouse nor observed chastity for God's sake but, moved by desire, have defiled your good name before God and man by the crime of adulterous lust, then we are greatly grieved because this is a sin in the sight of God and is the ruin of your fair fame among men.

And now, what is worse, our informants say that these atrocious crimes are committed in convents with holy nuns and virgins consecrated to God, and this, beyond all doubt, doubles the offense. Let us take, by way of illustration, the punishment due to a rascal who has committed adultery with the wife of his lord and consider how much more he deserves who has defiled a bride of Christ, the Creator of heaven and earth, with his filthy lust; as Paul the Apostle says: "Know ye not that your bodies are temples of the Holy Spirit?" and also: "Know ye not that ye are the temple of God, and that the spirit of God dwelleth in you? If any man shall defile the temple of God, him shall God destroy; for the temple of God is holy, which temple ye are." And again, in his discourse and enumeration of sins he classes fornicators and adulterers together: "Know ye not that the unrighteous shall not inherit the kingdom of God? Be not deceived: neither fornicators, nor idolaters, nor adulterers, nor effeminate, nor abusers of themselves with mankind, nor thieves, nor covetous, nor drunkards, nor revilers, nor extortioners, shall inherit the kingdom of God." Among the Greeks and Romans—as if one accused of this were charged with blasphemy against God—special inquiry is made before ordination regarding it, and if the man be found guilty of intercourse with a veiled nun consecrated to God, he is absolutely excluded from every grade of God's priesthood.

On this account, beloved son, one should consider what a heavy sin this is held to be in the sight of the Eternal Judge, so that it places the guilty one among the slaves of idolatry and shuts him out from the ministry of the altar, even though he has made his peace with God by previous acts of penitence. The bodies which are consecrated to Him by our own vows and by the words of the priest are said by Holy Scripture to be temples of God, wherefore those who violate them are shown to be sons of perdition according to the Apostle. Peter, prince of the Apostles, in his prohibitions against lust says: "For the time past may suffice," etc. Also: "The price of a harlot is scarcely that of one piece of bread, but a woman steals the precious soul of a man." Again: "It is no great fault if a man steal; for he steals to satisfy his hunger, and if he is caught he makes seven-fold restitution. But the adulterer loses his soul through his lack of understanding." It would be a long story to tell how many physicians of the soul have declaimed against the horrible poison of this sin and forbidden it with terrible threats; for fornication is worse than almost any other sin and may truly be described as a snare of death, an abyss of hell, and a whirlpool of perdition.

We therefore, beloved son, beseech Your Grace by Christ the son of God and by His coming and by His kingdom, that if it is true that you are continuing in this vice you will amend your life by penitence, purify yourself, and bear in mind how vile a thing it is through lust to change the image of God created in you into the image and likeness of a vicious demon. Remember that you were made king and ruler over many not by your own merits but by the abounding grace of God, and now you are making yourself by your own lust the slave of an evil spirit, since, as the Apostle says, whatever sin a man commits, of that he becomes the slave.

This is held to be a shame and disgrace, not by Christians only but even by pagans. For the pagans themselves, although ignorant of the true God, keep in this matter the substance of the law and the ordinance of God from the beginning, inasmuch as they respect their wives with the bond of matrimony and punish fornicators and adulterers. In Old Saxony, if a virgin disgraces her father's house by adultery or if a married woman breaks the bond of wedlock and commits adultery, they sometimes compel her to hang herself with her own hand and then hang the seducer above the pyre on which she has been burned. Sometimes a troop of women get together and flog her through the towns, beating her with rods and stripping her to the waist, cutting her whole body with knives, pricking her with wounds, and sending her on bleeding and torn from town to town; fresh scourgers join in with new zeal for purity, until finally they leave her dead or almost dead, that other women may be made to fear adultery and evil conduct. The Wends, who are the vilest and lowest race of men, have such high regard for the mutual bond of marriage that the wife refuses to survive her husband. Among them a woman is praised who dies by her own hand and is burned upon the same pyre with her husband.

If, then, heathen who know not God and have not the law do, as the Apostle says, by nature the things of the law and have the works of the law written upon their hearts, know you, beloved son, who are called a Christian and a worshipper of the true God —if in your youth you were ensnared in the filth of wantonness and involved in the mire of adultery and sunk in the whirlpool of lust as in an abyss of hell—it is now high time that you should remember your Lord, should rouse yourself from the snares of the devil, and wash your soul clean from the filthiness of lust. It is time for you in fear of your Creator no longer to venture to defile yourself by repeating such sins. It is time for you to have mercy upon the multitude of your people who are perishing by following the example of a sinful prince and are falling into the abyss of death. For, beyond a doubt, we shall receive from the eternal judge rewards for as many as we lead by good example into the life of our heavenly fatherland, and punishment for those whom we guide by evil example into perdition.

If the English people, as is reported here and as is charged against us in France and Italy and even by the heathen themselves, are scorning lawful marriage and living in wanton adultery like the people of Sodom, then we must expect that a degenerate and degraded people with unbridled desires will be produced. At last the whole race will become debased and finally will be neither strong in war nor steadfast in faith, neither honored among men nor pleasing in the sight of God. So it has been with the peoples of Spain and Provence and Burgundy. They turned thus away from God and lived in harlotry until the Almighty Judge let the penalties for such crimes fall upon them through ignorance of the law of God and the coming of the Saracens.

It must further be noted that in this crime another frightful sin is involved, namely murder. For when those harlots, be they nuns or not, bring forth their offspring conceived in sin, they generally kill them and so, instead of filling the churches of Christ with children of adoption, they crowd tombs with corpses and hell with miserable souls.

It is further reported to us that you have destroyed many privileges of churches and deprived them of some of their property. If that is true, it is a very grave offense, as Holy Scripture testifies: "He who steals from his father or mother, saying, 'This is no crime,' is partner in a homicide." Surely God who created us is our father, and the Church which has re-created us spiritually by baptism is our mother. Therefore he who steals or gains by fraud the goods of Christ and the Church shall be called a homicide in the sight of the righteous judge. Of him a certain wise man said: "He who steals his neighbor's money commits a crime, but he who steals the money of the Church commits a sacrilege."

It is said also that your governors and earls treat monks with greater violence and extortion than any Christian kings have ever done before. Ever since Saint Gregory, apostolic pontiff, sent preachers of the catholic faith from the Apostolic See and converted the English to the true God, the privileges of the churches in the English realm remained undisturbed and inviolate until the time of Ceolred, king of Mercia, and Osred, king of Deira and Bernicia. These two kings, inspired by the devil, made public display of these two most grievous sins through the lands of the English in defiance of the commands of the Gospel and the apostolic teachings of our Savior. Persisting in these crimes, that is, in the adulterous violation of nuns and the destruction of monasteries, they were condemned by the righteous justice of God and cast down from their royal state, overtaken by an early and terrible death, shut out from the light eternal, and plunged into the depths of hell. Ceolred, the predecessor of Your Reverend Highness, as it was told by those who were present, while he sat feasting amidst his companions was suddenly stricken in his sins with madness by an evil spirit, who had seduced him by his persuasions into rash defiance of the law of God. So without repentance or confession, raving mad, talking with devils and cursing the priests of God, he passed on, without doubt, from this life to the torments of hell. Osred also, driven by a spirit of license, pursued consecrated virgins in their convents, with furious violence, until he lost his glorious kingdom, his young life, and his lustful soul by a miserable and shameful death.

Wherefore, beloved son, beware the pit into which you have seen others fall before you! Beware the darts of the ancient foe by which you have seen your own relatives wounded and slain! Guard yourself against the snares of him who lies in wait for you, whereby you have seen your friends and companions entrapped with the loss of their lives here and hereafter. Follow not the example of such to your own ruin. Such are they who, according to Holy Writ, have oppressed the righteous and taken away their works. In the day of judgment they will say: "We have strayed from the path of truth, and the light of righteousness has not shone for us and the sun has not risen upon us. . . ."[1]

The riches of this world are of no avail in the day of requital if a man comes to the end of his life while still making bad use of them; for after the death of the body he shall fall into eternal punishment of the soul. Take these warnings to heart, my dear son, and, I pray you, yield to the prudent words of God's law and reform your life. Turn away from your vices and make an effort to acquire the sacred virtues; so shall you prosper in this world and receive eternal reward in the world to come.

May Almighty God so turn your life to better things that you may be worthy of the grace of our Lord himself forevermore.

LVIII [74]. *Boniface to a priest, Herefrid, concerning his letter to King Ethelbald* [746–747]

To his beloved and reverend brother, the priest Herefrid, Boniface, servant of the servants of God, sends greetings of undying love in Christ.

I most earnestly beg your gracious friendship to be mindful of me in your holy prayers although, from the accounts of those who

---

[1] Long quotations from the Book of Wisdom, Ecclesiasticus, Matthew, and James are here omitted.

come from you, I have no doubt that you have done so and will continue so to do. May the words of St. James the Apostle be fulfilled in us, where he says: "Pray for one another that ye may be healed," and: "The earnest prayer of the righteous man availeth much."

We eight bishops, whose names are given below, meeting together, urgently request you, our dearest brother, to convey to Ethelbald, king of the Mercians, our letter of admonition, to read it to him with your explanations, and, in the same form and order in which we wrote and sent it to you, to call his attention to each point with your exhortations. For we have heard that in your fear of God you fear not the person of man and that at times the said king has been willing to give some little heed to your warnings. Let Your Goodness be assured that these admonitory words of ours were sent to that king from no other motive than pure affection for him and because, being born and bred of that same English stock, we sojourn here by the orders of the Apostolic See. The well-doing and the fair fame of our race is our joy and delight; their sins and their evil repute fill us with grief and sorrow. We suffer from the disgrace of our people whether it be told by Christians or pagans that the English race reject the usages of other peoples and the apostolic commands—nay, the ordinance of God— and refuse to hold to one wife, basely defiling and mixing up everything with their adulterous lusts, like whinnying horses or braying asses.

Wherefore, beloved brother, if this, the greatest of vices, really exists, let us all with one accord urge the king to reform himself and his people with him, lest the whole race perish with its prince both here and in the life to come. Let him amend his own life and, by his example, guide his people into the way of salvation, so that whereas before he incurred guilt he may henceforth merit an eternal reward.

We are sending you, as a token of sincere affection and of our blessing, a napkin with a little incense. May the Holy Trinity preserve you in lasting health and in all holy endeavor as you go forward in the way of your well-proven character.

LIX [75]. *Boniface to Archbishop Egbert of York concerning his
letter to King Ethelbald* [746–747]

To his dear and reverend brother, Archbishop Egbert, Boniface,
servant of the servants of God and legate of the Apostolic See in
Germany, sends sincere greetings of spiritual brotherhood in Christ.

When I received your gifts and books I lifted up my hands and
gave thanks to Almighty God who has given me such a friend in
my long wanderings, to help me in my worldly affairs and comfort
me with his prayers and the divine solace of spiritual communion.
And now, from the depths of my heart I beg your gracious friendship to admit me and the servants of God who labor with me into
the company of your brotherhood and that you will be my adviser
and helper in my researches into the rules of the Church regarding
the judgments of God. Be assured that I am not using trifling
words but am asking in all seriousness, not in pride or arrogance,
or following my own opinion more than I ought. The Catholic
and Apostolic Church of Rome, in sending me as an unworthy and
humble preacher to the erring or pagan peoples of Germany, enjoined upon me by authority of the Roman pontiff that if, as I
went among Christians, I should find people in error, or church
rules perverted by evil practices, or men led away from the catholic faith into pathless ways, I should strive with all my strength
to call them back into the way of salvation.

Desiring to follow this precept, I sent a letter of exhortation
and admonition to Ethelbald, king of Mercia, with the advice and
consent of the bishops who are working with me. I ordered this
letter to be shown to you for inspection so that you might correct
whatever you found wrong in it and might flavor with the spice of
your wisdom and strengthen by your authority whatever was right.
Also, if you should see that the roots of those evils described in the
letter against the king of Mercia are springing up among your own
people, you might cut them down in time like a wise and prudent
husbandman with the reaping hook of the Lord's authority and
root them out completely, lest "their vine be of the vine of Sodom

and of the fields of Gomorrah and their wine be the poison of dragons and the cruel venom of asps." It is an evil unheard of in times past and, as servants of God here versed in the Scriptures say, three or four times worse than the corruption of Sodom, if a Christian people should turn against lawful marriage contrary to the practice of the whole world—nay, to the divine command—and should give itself over to incest, lust, and adultery, and the seduction of veiled and consecrated women.

I beg you also to have copied and sent to me some of the treatises of the lector Bede whom, as we learn, divine grace has endowed with spiritual intelligence and permitted to shine forth in your country, so that we too may profit by the light of that torch which the Lord has granted unto you.

Meanwhile, as a token of fraternal love, I am sending you a copy of some letters of St. Gregory which I have obtained from the archives of the Roman Church, and which, so far as I know, have not yet reached Britain.

If you so order, I will send more, as I have received many of them. I am sending also a cloak and a towel for drying after washing the feet of the servants of God.

We pray that Your Holiness may keep your health and go onward in holy virtue.

LX [76]. *Boniface requests Abbot Huetbert of Wearmouth to send him some of the works of Bede*   [746–747]

To his very dear and reverend brother, Abbot Huetbert, and to all the brethren of his holy community, Boniface, a humble servant of the servants of God, sends greeting of brotherly love in Christ.

We earnestly beseech your brotherly piety to aid us with your most holy prayers as we labor among the ignorant and savage peoples of Germany, planting the seeds of the Gospel, so that by the prayers of Your Holiness the raging heat of these Babylonian flames may be held in check and the seed strewn in the furrows may spring up into manifold fruition. For, in the words of the Apostle, "Neither is he that planteth anything, neither he that watereth; but God that giveth the increase"; and, "Utterance may be given unto me in opening my mouth"; and, "That the word of the Lord may run and be glorified." Meantime we beg you to be so kind as to copy and send us some of the treatises of that keenest investigator of the Scriptures, the monk Bede, who, we have learned, shone forth among you of late as a lantern of the Church, by his scriptural scholarship.

If it would not give you too much trouble, pray send us a cloak, which would be a great comfort in our journeys.

As a token of our deep affection we are sending you a coverlet, as they call them here, made of goats' hair, and beg you to accept it, trifle though it is, as a reminder of me.

May the blessed Trinity, One God, guard you and prosper you in health and every holy virtue in this life, and glorify and reward you in future blessedness among the shining cohorts of angels.

LXI [77]. *Pope Zacharias informs Boniface that he has sent copies of certain canons to Pippin*   Jan. 5, 747

Zacharias, servant of the servants of God, to Boniface, his very reverend and holy brother and fellow bishop.

The noble and blessed Apostle Paul bids us: "Be ye followers of me even as I also am of Christ"; wherefore, though absent in body, we are ever present to Your Brotherly Holiness in spirit through the bond of spiritual affection. We hold you in the depths of our heart as a beloved brother and fellow priest and, sinner though we be, yet trusting in a divine hope we cease not to keep the memory of you in our prayers, begging the unmeasured divinity of Christ our God to strengthen you in doing his service, so that in the day of His coming you may be able to speak that word of comfort: "Lo, here am I and the children thou hast given me;

I have not lost a single one of them." And straightway that sublime and welcome word shall summon you into the company of those who from the beginning of the world have been pleasing unto him: "Come, ye blessed of my father, inherit the kingdom prepared for you from the foundation of the world."

Be it known to you, beloved, that the most noble Pippin, palace mayor of the Frankish people, sent us an urgent request by a man of his, the pious priest Ardobanius, that we should send him certain chapters of the law regarding the priestly order and others concerning the salvation of souls, as also concerning unlawful marriage, and how these were to be observed in accordance with the ritual of the Christian religion and the sacred canons. Although Your Holiness has already a thorough knowledge of our decisions upon these matters, we gave ear to his wishes and sent him a brief summary of the apostolic documents. We gave also therewith instructions that they were to be read in the assembly of priests and that Your Holiness was to be asked to be there.

When a synod shall be held to discuss these matters, let those blasphemous and obstinate ex-bishops, Aldebert, Godalsacius, and Clemens, be brought in and their case thoroughly sifted in a final careful investigation. If you find that they have wandered from the right way but are inclined to turn back into the path of rectitude, do you, in conjunction with the prince of that province, dispose of the case as shall seem best to you, according to the sacred canons. But if they shall obstinately persist in their stubborn pride and declare themselves not guilty, then send them on to us with two or three approved and trusty priests, that their case may be inquired into before the Apostolic See and that they may receive the final sentence they deserve. So act, beloved brother, in the ministry entrusted to you that you may receive a reward from Almighty God and may merit eternal life.

May God keep you safe, most reverend and holy brother.

Given the Nones of January in the twenty-eighth year of our most pious and august Lord Constantine, crowned emperor by God, in the sixth year of his consulship, in the fifteenth indiction.

LXII [78]. *Boniface to Archbishop Cuthbert of Canterbury;
report of Frankish synods; complaints of obstacles to his
mission*   [747]

To his brother and fellow bishop, Cuthbert, raised to the dignity
of the archiepiscopate and joined to him by the bond of spiritual
kinship, Boniface, legate for Germany of the Catholic and Apostolic Church of Rome, sends greetings of intimate love in Christ.

It is written in the Book of Solomon: "Happy is the man who
finds a friend with whom he can talk as with himself." We have received by the hand of your son, the deacon Kunibert, together with
your generous gifts, a delightful and affectionate letter. You have
also kindly sent me by him verbally a welcome discourse concerning our fraternal relations. We hope that as long as life shall last
this exchange of spiritual counsel may go on if God will, from
whom alone "all holy desires, all good counsel, and all just works
do proceed." May you and we be bound together in the golden
bonds of heavenly love which cannot be broken—you better and
more fully because God has endowed you with greater gifts of
knowledge and power, we striving to be instructed as your devoted
vassal "faithful over a few things."

The work of our ministry is in one and the same cause, and an
equal oversight of churches and people is entrusted to us, whether
in teaching or in restraining or in admonition or in protecting all
classes of the clergy or the laity. Wherefore I humbly request
that if at any time God shall inspire you or your synods with
wholesome counsel you will not hesitate to share it with us. And
we likewise, if God shall impart to our infirmity anything useful
or acceptable to you, will do the same by you. Our responsibility
toward churches and peoples is greater than that of other bishops
on account of the pallium entrusted to us and accepted by us, while
they have the care of their own dioceses only. And hence, dear
friend—not that you, who are so wise, need to hear or read the
decisions of us simple folk—we feel that on account of your holy
and humble good will toward us you would prefer to be informed
about what we here have decided and now submit to you for correction and improvement.

We have determined in our synod: that we shall maintain the catholic faith and unity and our subjection to the Roman Church as long as we live; that we shall be the willing subjects of St. Peter and of his Vicar; that we shall hold a synod every year; that our metropolitan bishops shall ask for their palliums from that See; and that in all things we shall obey the orders of St. Peter according to the canons, so that we may be counted among the sheep entrusted to his care. To these declarations we have all agreed and subscribed, and we have forwarded them to the shrine of St. Peter, prince of the Apostles. The Roman clergy and the pontiff have gratefully accepted them.

We have determined that every year the canonical decrees, the laws of the Church, and the Rule of the regular life shall be read and renewed at the synod. We have ordered that the metropolitan, having received his pallium, shall exhort the other bishops, admonish them, and make inquiry as to who among them is watchful of the people's welfare and who is negligent. We have forbidden the servants of God to hunt, to go about in the woods with dogs, and to keep hawks or falcons. We have ordered that every priest annually during Lent shall render to his bishop an account of his ministry, the state of the catholic faith, baptism, and every detail of his administration. We have decreed that every bishop shall make the rounds of his diocese annually, confirming and instructing the people, seeking out and forbidding pagan rites, divination, fortune-telling, soothsaying, charms, incantations, and all Gentile vileness. We have forbidden the servants of God to wear showy or martial dress or to carry arms.

We have determined that it shall be the special duty of the metropolitan to inquire into the conduct of the bishops under him and their care for the people. He shall require them, upon their return from the synod, each to hold a meeting in his own diocese with his priests and abbots and urge them to carry out the synodal decrees. And every bishop finding himself unable to reform or correct some fault in his own diocese shall lay the case openly in the synod before the archbishop for correction, just as the Roman Church, at my ordination, bound me by an oath that if I should find priests or people wandering from the law of God and could not correct them, I would always faithfully report the case to the Apostolic See and the Vicar of St. Peter for settlement. Thus, if I am not mistaken, should every bishop do to his metropolitan, and he to the Roman pontiff, if the case cannot be settled among themselves. So shall they be guiltless of the blood of lost souls.

Furthermore, dear brother, our labor is the same but our responsibility greater than that of other priests. The ancient canons prescribe, as everyone knows, that the metropolitan is to have charge of a whole province, and I fear that we have, so to speak, undertaken to steer a ship through the waves of an angry sea and can neither control it nor without sin abandon it—for, as a certain wise man says:

If it is dangerous to be negligent in steering a ship in the midst of the sea, how much more perilous to abandon it in a storm with the waves running high; and even so the Church which makes its way through the ocean of this world like a great ship, buffeted in this life by diverse waves of temptation, is yet not to be abandoned but to be controlled.[1]

As examples we have the early fathers Clement and Cornelius and many others in Rome, Cyprian in Carthage, Athanasius in Alexandria, who, under pagan emperors, guided the ship of Christ—nay, his dearest spouse, the Church—teaching, defending, laboring, and suffering even unto the shedding of blood. Of myself I can surely say in the words of the Song of Songs: "The sons of my mother have fought against me. They set me as a watchman in the vineyards, and my own vineyard I have not kept." For the vineyard, according to Nahum, the prophet of the Lord of Sabaoth, is the House of Israel, now the Church Catholic. I have undertaken to bring together and to instruct a synod, by command of the Roman pontiff and with the sanction of the princes of the Franks and Gauls, in the hope of reconstructing the law of Christ in that Church. I have dug the ground round about, I have enriched it with manure, but I have not guarded it. While I waited for it to bear grapes, it brought forth wild grapes, and, according to another prophet: "The labor of the olive shall fail, and the fields shall yield no meat." But, alas! My labor seems like that of a barking dog that sees thieves and robbers break in and plunder his master's

---

[1] Julianus Pomerius, *De vita contemplativa;* Migne, *P. L.,* 59, 431.

house, but, because he has none to help him in his defense, can only whine and complain.

But now, being in such a position and asking your wholesome advice as to what seems right and prudent, I suggest that it is time to speak freely. I say, as the Apostle Paul said in the Acts of the Apostles:

Wherefore I take you to record this day, that I am pure from the blood of all men. For I have not shunned to declare unto you all the counsel of God. Take heed, therefore, unto yourselves and to all the flock over the which the Holy Ghost hath made you overseers to feed the Church of God, which he hath purchased with his own blood.

He says: "I have walked among you preaching the kingdom of God that I might keep myself guiltless of the destruction of all." The Apostle calls the priest "bishop," the prophet calls him "watchman," and the Savior of the world calls him "shepherd of the Church." They all agree that the teacher and guide who hides the sins of the people in silence becomes thereby guilty of the blood of lost souls.

For this reason a dread necessity impels us to present ourselves as an example to the faithful according to the word of the Apostle—that is, if I am not mistaken, the teacher is to live so justly that his deeds shall not contradict his words and that, while he himself may live prudently, he shall not be silently condemned for the sins of others. He is set over the Church of God to this end, that he not only may set an example of right living to others, but, through his dutiful preaching, may bring every man's sins before his eyes and show him what punishment awaits the hard of heart and what reward the obedient. For, according to the word of God to Ezekiel, he to whom the preaching of the word is entrusted, even though he live a holy life, nevertheless, if he is afraid or ashamed to rebuke those who live wickedly, shall perish, together with all those who perish through his silence. And what shall it profit him to escape the penalty of his own sins if he is to be punished for those of others?

[Here follows a long passage, chiefly occupied by quotations from the Scripture, especially from Ezekiel and Paul, enforcing the same idea of the responsibility of bishops.]

Finally, I will not conceal from Your Grace that all the servants of God here who are especially versed in Scripture and strong in the fear of God are agreed that it would be well and favorable for the honor and purity of your church, and provide a certain shield against vice, if your synod and your princes would forbid matrons and veiled women to make these frequent journeys back and forth to Rome. A great part of them perish and few keep their virtue. There are very few towns in Lombardy or Frankland[1] or Gaul where there is not a courtesan or a harlot of English stock. It is a scandal and a disgrace to your whole church.

As to the point that any layman, be he emperor, king, official, or count, relying upon secular force, may capture a monastery from the power of a bishop, an abbot, or an abbess and begin to rule there in the place of an abbot, have monks under him, and hold property bought by the blood of Christ—the ancient fathers called such a man a robber, sacrilegious, a murderer of the poor, a devil's wolf entering the sheepfold of Christ, to be condemned with the ultimate anathema before the judgment seat of Christ. Remember the words of St. Paul the Apostle about such men, saying to Timothy: "Charge them that are rich in this world, that they be not high-minded, nor trust in uncertain riches, but in the living God, who giveth us richly all things to enjoy." If such receive not the correction of the Church, they are heathen and publicans, and the Church of God refuses to them, either alive or dead, all communion. Against such men let us sound the trumpet of God that we be not condemned for our silence.

Strive with all your might against foolish superstition in dress, a thing hateful to God. Those ornaments, as they call them, but which others call foulness, with their wide, embroidered purple stripes, are sent by Antichrist to herald his coming. Through his craftiness he introduces into monasteries by his own servants fornication and lust,[2] sinful friendships of youths in purple garments,

---

[1] *Francia.* From the use of the terms Lombardy and Gaul, it would seem that Boniface probably had East Francia in mind.

[2] In MSS 1, 3, and 6 the text ends here. The continuation is found only in the records of the recipient. *See* Spelman, *Concilia orbis Britannici*, I, 237.

distaste for study or prayer, and the ruin of souls. Such attire shows the nakedness of their souls, giving proof of arrogance, pride, luxury, and vanity, of which Wisdom says: "Pride, and arrogancy, and the evil way, and the froward mouth, do I hate." It is said also that the vice of drunkenness is far too common in your parishes and that some bishops not only do not prohibit it, but themselves drink to the point of intoxication and, by offering very large drinks to others, force them into drunkenness. There can be no doubt that this is a grave offense in any servant of God, for the canons of the fathers order a drunken bishop or priest to reform or be degraded. And the Truth itself says: "Take heed to yourselves, lest at any time your hearts be overcharged with surfeiting and drunkenness." And St. Paul: "Be not drunk with wine, wherein is excess." And the prophet Isaiah: "Woe unto them that are mighty to drink wine, and men of strength to mingle strong drink." This is an evil peculiar to the heathen and to our race, for neither the Franks, nor the Gauls, nor the Lombards, nor the Romans, nor the Greeks practice it. Let us, if possible, put a check upon it by synodal action and the commands of Scripture. At all events, by avoiding it ourselves and prohibiting it we shall deliver our souls from the blood of the damned.

As to the forced labor of monks upon royal buildings and other works, a thing unheard of anywhere excepting only in England, let not the priests of God keep silence or consent thereto. It is an evil unknown in times gone by.

May God's hand preserve you safe, reverend and beloved brother, against all adversity, to make intercession for us.

LXIII [79]. *An anonymous letter to one Andhemus inquiring about Boniface* [747–748]

To his beloved father, Andhemus, in the bonds of love in Christ, profound greetings.

Why have you not sent the clothes you were to send from Frisia? Now, in the name of God Almighty, make haste and see that they come!

Let us have word about our bishop [Boniface], whether he has gone to a synod of the duke [Pippin] of the western provinces [Neustria] or to the son of Karlmann [Drogo]. Send word to us in writing. Send back at once this messenger named Hardleih, who is hurrying to you. I beg you, Sir, to protect him while he stays and on his return journey.

Farewell, O blossom of the Church! Pray for us as we for you, and may the peace of Christ abide in us. Amen.

LXIV [80]. *Pope Zacharias to Boniface, reviewing the questions of baptism, heresy, and the Frankish synods*   May 1, 748

Zacharias, servant of the servants of God, to Boniface, his very reverend and holy brother and fellow bishop.

Our beloved Bishop Burchard, presenting himself at the threshold of the blessed Peter, prince of the Apostles, and coming to us, has brought an address from Your Fraternal Holiness. From this we learn that you are having a hard fight in your strenuous work of preaching the Gospel of Christ our God and upholding the holy catholic, orthodox and genuine faith received from our Redeemer, God, and Lord Jesus Christ and handed down through the blessed Peter, His own appointed prince of the Apostles, and Paul, His chosen vessel, and all the Apostles. Hearing this we, sinner though we are, lifted up our hands to Almighty God and returned our boundless thanks, beseeching His ineffable divinity to confirm and strengthen your courage still more and keep you safe and sound in body so long as He shall bid you live. May you accomplish the mission laid upon you for the winning of souls against the day of Jesus Christ, that you may be worthy to hear that word of welcome which the Lord will speak to those who love him: "Come, ye blessed of my Father, inherit the kingdom prepared for you from the foundation of the world."

In this address of yours there were also several topics as to which you urgently requested the judgment, the advice, and the comfort of the Apostolic See.

First, touching the synod of the church within which you were born and brought up, among the people of the Anglo-Saxons in the island of Britain. Over this church the first preachers sent out by the Apostolic See—Augustine, Laurentius, Justus, Honorius, and recently, within your own time, the Greco-Roman Theodorus, once a learned philosopher at Athens, then ordained and given the pallium at Rome and sent on to Britain—presided and gave decisions. Therein it was decreed and strictly ordered and faithfully observed that whoever was baptized without the invocation of the Trinity did not receive the sacrament of regeneration. And that is absolutely true; for if one is immersed in the font of baptism without the invocation of the Trinity, he has gained nothing unless he be baptized in the name of the Father and of the Son and of the Holy Spirit.

You write also about those who hold that if one be immersed with the words of the Gospel and the invocation of the Trinity in the name of the Father, the Son, and the Holy Spirit, he undoubtedly receives the sacrament, so that even if such baptism were administered to him who asks for it by a heretic or schismatic, or by a thief or a robber or an adulterer, it would, nevertheless, be the baptism of Christ infallibly consecrated by the Gospel words. On the contrary, baptism administered even by a righteous man, if he has not called upon the Trinity at the font according to the Lord's appointment, such baptism as he gives is not a real one. Now as to those base and impure heretics and schismatics who baptize those who request it in the name of the Trinity and also those who, without invocation of the Trinity, immerse in the baptismal font, you, my brother, know what is contained in the sacred canons about these, and we exhort you to hold fast thereby. It is written in the Lord's word: "Be ye holy, even as I am holy." Stand firmly by what you received from our predecessor, Gregory of blessed memory. Fall not away in the least from the tradition of the Gospels and the Apostles as handed down by the holy fathers, but armed with the breastplate of faith and the helmet of salvation, fight manfully against the iniquity of diabolical deceitfulness by setting forth the apostolic life. For it is written: "Behold I have made thy face strong against their faces, and I will comfort thy steadfastness against their assaults, and thy steadfastness shall be firmer than a rock."

As to those sacrilegious priests who, you say, sacrificed bulls and goats to heathen gods, eating the offerings to the dead, defiling their own ministry, and who are now dead, so that it cannot be known whether they invoked the Trinity in their baptisms or not, while the survivors are in fear lest they be not truly baptized by such a ceremony, you have ordered that all should be rebaptized. In the above-mentioned synod the clergy took the same position, namely, that if any person of the Trinity were not named in baptism, this could not be a true baptism. And it is certainly true that he who has not confessed any one member of the Holy Trinity cannot be fully a Christian. For if he confesses the Father and the Son, but not the Holy Spirit, he then has neither the Father nor the Son; and he who confesses the Father and the Holy Spirit, but not the Son, has neither the Father nor the Holy Spirit, but is wholly without divine grace.

You report also, my brother, that you have found so-called priests, more in number than the true catholics, heretical pretenders under the name of bishops or priests but never ordained by catholic bishops. They lead the people astray and bring confusion into the service of the Church. Some are false vagrants, adulterers, murderers, effeminates, pederasts, blasphemers, hypocrites, and many of them are tonsured serfs who have fled from their masters, servants of the devil transformed into ministers of Christ, who, subject to no bishop, live according to their own caprice, protected by the people against the bishops, so that these have no check upon their scandalous conduct. They gather about them a like-minded following and carry on their false ministry, not in a catholic church, but in the open country in the huts of farm laborers, where their ignorance and stupid folly can be hidden from the bishops. They neither preach the catholic faith to pagans, nor have they themselves the true faith. They do not even know the sacred words which any catechumen old enough to use his reason can learn and understand, nor do they expect them to be uttered by those whom they are to baptize, as, for instance, the renunciation of Satan, and so forth. Neither do they fortify them with the sign of the cross, which should precede baptism, nor do they teach them belief in one God and the Holy Trinity; nor do they require them to believe with the heart for righteousness or to make confession with the lips for salvation.

Wherever, beloved, you find these ministers, not of Christ but of Satan, you will call a meeting of the clergy of the province and utterly reject them. You will strip them of their priestly functions and order them to spend their lives in penance under monastic rule. Thus disciplined in the body, if they ever turn to the right way and believe in their hearts, let a true confession with the lips witness to their salvation. But even if they shall not be converted, the justice of your decision shall not be denied. For you will have as your consolation against the iniquity of evildoers the canonical sanction of the holy Apostles and other recognized fathers.

Therefore, most reverend brother, be strong to win in the law, in the Gospel of Christ, and in the preaching of that catholic and orthodox faith which shall glorify you. For tribulation of our body is temporal and has an end, but "experience [hath] hope: and hope maketh not ashamed; because the love of God is shed abroad in our hearts by the Holy Ghost, which is given unto us. . . . Who shall separate us from the love of Christ? Shall tribulation or anguish?" and so forth. Though we be cast down, my brother, we shall not be destroyed. Let us bear about in our bodies the death of Jesus, that the life of Jesus may be manifest in our bodies in the day of his coming, as we are taught in His divine Word: "Blessed are they which are persecuted for righteousness' sake; for theirs is the kingdom of Heaven."

Encourage also all our beloved orthodox bishops, priests, deacons and clerks, pious abbots and monks, all glorious dukes and nobles who are defenders of the Christian law, to aid us against the enemies of the orthodox faith and all heretics and schismatics, that they may be worthy of reward for their good works in the kingdom of heaven, as it is written: "Him that overcometh I will make a pillar of my temple and will write my name upon him."

You say, my brother, that you have found a certain priest, a Scot by birth, named Sampson, who has wandered from the path of truth, saying that one may become a Christian through laying on of hands by a bishop, without the ritual invocation or the water of regeneration. He who says such a thing is devoid of the Holy Spirit and a stranger to the grace of Christ. He is to be cut off from the fellowship of the priesthood. For who can be a true catholic unless he be baptized according to the Lord's command in the name of the Father, the Son, and the Holy Spirit, and then consecrated by laying on of hands? After due condemnation, expel this scandalous person who says such things from the Holy Church of God.

But as to those who were baptized by heretics, where there is room for doubt whether or not they were baptized in the name of the Father, the Son, and the Holy Spirit, inquire carefully into the facts of the case to ascertain whether they were baptized by priests of unsound faith and fail not to deal with them according to the rules handed down to you by our predecessor, Pope Gregory of blessed memory, and the sacred canons, that they may not be lost forever but saved by consecration according to the Gospel.

We have examined the document which you sent out to all bishops, priests, deacons, and others leading the religious life, concerning the unity of the catholic faith and the apostolic teaching. Pray accept our most hearty commendation, beloved, for the zeal you have shown in doing this through the grace of the Holy Spirit vouchsafed to you.

You have asked in another letter, holy brother, that a clergyman may be sent by us to the regions of Gallia and Francia[1] to hold a synod there. But so long as, by the grace of God, Your Holiness is there to represent us and the Apostolic See, it is not necessary to send anyone else.

When you find men, my devoted brother, who have knowledge of the sacred doctrine, who keep the sacred law and defend the orthodox faith without hesitation, be diligent in sending them out to preach the word of salvation in such places as you may select.

[1] See note above, p. 111.

Bring together the bishops of your province and hold councils when and where you may think best, and if you find any in the way of error, shame them in such wise that they may be without honor before all men. The Lord our God will be with you.

We have received the written statement of the true orthodox faith and catholic unity which Your Reverence, together with our beloved bishops in Frankland, have sent us. As we opened it we were filled with joy and gave boundless thanks to God the Father Almighty who has deigned to bring them back into unity among themselves and harmony with us, that their spiritual mother, the Holy Church, may rejoice in them. Salute them all, beloved, in our stead, with the kiss of peace of Christ. We have sent them also an apostolic letter of thanks for their devotion.

Your Holiness has also informed us that that man Virgilius— we know not whether he is to be called priest—is abusing you because you convicted him of error in regard to the catholic doctrine and is making insinuations to Duke Odilo of Bavaria in order to sow dissension between the duke and you. He says that he was given by us the authorization, upon the death of one of those four bishops whom you ordained in that country, to take possession of the vacant diocese. That is absolutely false, a lie based on his own wickedness. As to the foolish and sinful doctrine which he teaches: if it should be made clear that he believes there is below this earth another world and other men, and also a sun and a moon, then summon a council, depose him from the office of priest, and cast him out of the Church. We have also, however, written to the duke and have sent a summons to Virgilius to present himself before us for a thorough investigation so that, if he be proved to be in error, he may be condemned according to canonical rule. "For they that sow wickedness, reap the same." And it is written: "Froward thoughts separate from God: and his power, when it is tried, reproveth the unwise."

We acknowledge the letter of Your Holiness regarding the priests Sidonius and the aforesaid Virgilius. We have written them in a threatening tone, as befitted the case; we have more confidence in your word than in theirs. If it shall please God to spare our life

we shall summon them to the Apostolic See by an apostolic letter,
as we said above. For you have taught them, and they have not
accepted your teaching. In them is the Scripture fulfilled:

He that teaches a fool is like one who patches an earthen pot. It is
easier to carry sand and salt and a block of iron than a man without
wit, foolish and impious; for he who is lacking in sense thinks up empty
notions, and the witless and wandering invent follies.

But do not therefore, my brother, let yourself be provoked to
wrath. When you find such people, be patient, admonish, insist,
argue, and reprove them that they may be turned from their errors
into the way of truth. So, if they are converted you will have saved
their souls, and if they persist in their obstinacy you will not lose
the reward of your service; but then have no communion with
them, according to the word of the Apostle.

Another letter of yours, my brother, reports what you had
already written, that the Franks have not kept their word about
the city of Cologne and that you are now residing at Mainz.

Further, in view of your advanced age and fullness of days and
your bodily infirmities, you ask that, with our approval, if you
can find another person you may place him in the see over which
you now preside, you yourself, beloved, remaining, as you have
been, legate and messenger of the Apostolic See. But we, God helping us, advise Your Reverend Holiness for the welfare of rational
souls, never to give up the chair of the holy church of Mainz which
you now hold by the will of Christ, that the word of the Lord may
be fulfilled in you: "He that shall endure unto the end, the same
shall be saved."

If, however, the Lord shall send you in answer to your petition
a thoroughly suitable man who can take over the responsibility
and cure of souls, you will ordain him bishop as your representative, and he shall take up everywhere it is needed the preaching
and the ministry of Christ entrusted to you, guiding and strengthening the Church of God.

So we beseech the Lord our Redeemer through the intervention
of his holy mother, our Lady Mary, ever virgin, and of Peter

and Paul, princes of the Apostles, that He may deign to preserve you, our holy brother, safe and whole to pray for us.

God keep you free from harm, most reverend and holy brother.

Given on the Kalends of May in the twenty-ninth year of our most pious and august Lord Constantine, crowned by God emperor, in the seventh year of his consulship, in the first indiction.

LXV [81]. *King Aelbwald of East Anglia to Boniface* [747–749]

To Archbishop Boniface, illustrious and reverend master, gifted with every honorable quality, Aelbwald, ruler by the grace of God over the East Anglians, together with the whole abbey and community of the servants of God in our country, beseeching Him who is enthroned on high with prayers day and night for the welfare of the churches, send greeting in the name of God, the rewarder of all.

First, we desire you to know how grateful we are that you remember our unworthiness in your holy prayers. As your kindness has given directions with the prompting of God in regard to the solemn celebration of the Mass and perseverance in prayers, so we in our feeble way are earnestly striving to carry them out. Your name is to be remembered forever in the seven-fold recitation of the office[1] of our monasteries, the number seven being often used to indicate perfection. And this being well ordered and, with God's help, the rules of the soul duly established and the conditions of the inner man provided for, we desire that the outward support of the earthly goods given into our possession by the bounty of God should be placed under the control of your good will, on condition, however, that you graciously cause the continual aid of your prayers to be given us in the churches of God. And, as Divine Providence has been pleased to set you as pastor over His people, so we are anxious to have the benefit of your patronage. Let the names of the dead and of those who enter the way of all flesh be published on both sides, as the time of year requires, so that the

---

[1] The seven parts of the office: matins, lauds, prime, tierce, sext, nones, vespers, compline.

God of gods and Lord of lords who established you in the office of bishop may be pleased to guide his people through you to a knowledge of the indivisible Trinity and of the unity in substance.

Farewell, and may you finish your course with happiness up to the last step.

S - U S[1]

Finally, dear father, we wish you to know that we have sent the bearer of these presents in all friendliness, and, as we have found him loyal to you, so you will find him in all ways disposed to tell the truth to us.

LXVI [82]. *Pope Zacharias exhorts the leading Frankish bishops to follow the directions of Boniface*   [May 1, 748]

Zacharias, by the grace of God pontiff of the Apostolic See and servant of the servants of God, sends greeting in the Lord to his beloved Reginfrid, bishop of Rouen, Deodatus of Beauvais, Rimbert of Amiens, Eliseus of Noyon, Fulcher of Tongres, David of Speyer, Aetherius of Térouanne, Treward of Cambrai, Burchard of Würzburg, Genebaud of Laon, Romanus of Meaux, Agilulf of Cologne, Heddo of Strasburg and others, his devoted auxiliary bishops (*chorepiscopi*),[2] priests, and deacons and all orthodox clerks of the churches of God who hold to the apostolic doctrine.

I give thanks to God the Father Almighty and our Lord Jesus Christ His only Son and to the Holy Spirit, who has deigned to inspire all your hearts by the grace which He has poured out upon you so that you may walk in the unity of the faith and in the bond of peace; and may the glory of the Lord our God be upon you and abounding grace of peace and love, that you may be one body with your spiritual mother, the Holy Catholic and Apostolic Church of God, over which we preside by the ordinance of God. May you

---

[1] Wanting in the best manuscripts. It may be an abbreviation for *subscripsi*.

[2] The term "chorepiscopi," applied to ordinary bishops, is more than unusual in pontifical documents. Probably the original reading was "coepiscopi" (fellow bishops), which occurs constantly in papal correspondence.

fulfill that prophetic word: "Behold how good and how pleasant it is for brethren to dwell together in unity."

Though we are widely separated by distance, yet in the spirit of love we are ever present with you, holding you in our heart's depths and praying earnestly that our God and Lord Jesus Christ may still further support and strengthen your hearts to preach the Gospel in that ministry in which you serve, so that the people intrusted to you may be safely delivered from the snares of the devil through your pious admonitions and the help of God, and that you may be rewarded for the saving of their souls in the day of Christ. For it is written: "The sons of wisdom are the assembly of the righteous and their people are obedience and love. . . . I therefore beseech you, beloved, that ye walk worthy of the vocation wherewith ye are called, as is fitting for the saints, forbearing one another in love, endeavoring to keep the unity of the Spirit in the bond of peace" and love; for "the end of the commandment is charity out of a pure heart, and of a good conscience and of faith unfeigned."

I rejoice in you, beloved, because your faith and unity are precious to us and are shown, not only before God but also before men, since you have turned with abundant good will to your patron and master ordained of God, the blessed Peter, prince of the Apostles. Praised be your faith and your good reputation because you know what it is right to know. And now, with God's help, Your Holiness is joined with us in one fold and we have one shepherd, who was ordained by the Shepherd of shepherds, our Lord God and Savior, Jesus Christ, as prince of the Apostles and our teacher.

You have in our stead to strengthen your devotion and to labor with you for the Gospel our very holy and reverend brother, Archbishop Boniface, legate of the Apostolic See and our personal representative. Be constant, therefore, against the assaults of those who are wise in opposition but not in the things that are of God, and your constancy shall be firmer than a rock, as it is written: "Fear not before those who slay the body but cannot kill the soul." That which you hear in your ear proclaim in the light, fearing him who can slay both body and soul and send them to Gehenna.

Brethren, "though we walk in the flesh, we do not war after the flesh: For the weapons of our warfare are not carnal, but mighty through God to the pulling down of strongholds; defeating plans, casting down imaginations, and every high thing that exalteth itself against the knowledge of God, and bringing into captivity every thought to the obedience of Christ."

Finally, my brethren, "be strong in the Lord and in the power of his might." Peace and grace from God and our Lord Jesus Christ be with you abundantly. We embrace you, beloved, with the kiss of affection as if we were present with you, in the unity of spirit and in the bond of peace.

The Lord keep you unharmed, beloved.

LXVII [83]. *Pope Zacharias to certain Frankish noblemen and other people* [748]

Pope Zacharias to his noble sons, Throand, Sandrad, Nanther, Liutfried, Sterfried, Gundpert, Agnus, Haaldus, Rantulf, Robert, Brunichus, Rothard, Rocgonus, and to all, both high and low, bond and free.

I give thanks to God and the Lord Jesus Christ, only son of the Father, and to the Holy Spirit which guides your Christian faith, strengthening your hearts to walk in His commandments and to obey His precepts. When your loyalty and your good way of life were reported to us, as also your love toward your spiritual mother, the Holy Catholic and Apostolic Church of God, and for her priests, we rejoiced greatly and were joyful in the Lord. Sinful though we be, we implore His power to support and strengthen your hearts to do His will, that you may be worthy to receive in the kingdom of heaven that plentiful share of the fruits of your well-doing which God has prepared for those who love Him.

I admonish you, my beloved sons, to cherish the precepts of the Lord, His testimonies and His judgments. Do what is good and pleasing before the Lord, that it may be well with you, believing nothing else than what the Lord has spoken in the most holy

Gospels and what is contained in the ordinances of the holy and accepted canons. Lend not your ears to false priests or to those who utter falsehoods, coming to you in sheep's clothing but being inwardly ravening wolves. Put your trust rather in those who walk in the royal road and declare unto you the orthodox catholic faith, that your obedience may be acceptable in the sight of our Lord, according to the word of the Apostle: "Abhorring evil and cleaving only to that which is good," despising the things of this world and loving the things that are of God, that the treasure of your faith may shine forth in all things and your conversation be of good repute in heaven and upon earth. For you are not ignorant of the words of Scripture: "Abraham feared God, and it was counted to him for righteousness."

I enjoin upon you, beloved, to fear God and honor your priests, rendering them what is due to their holiness, that with your aid they may be strong to preach the word of salvation, safe and unmolested, and to preserve the government of the Church in vigor, that all the clergy may be subject to their bishops and may be taught by them in the sacred writings. For it is the Lord's command: "Render unto Caesar the things that are Caesar's and unto God the things that are God's."

I remind you of the apostolic teaching that no layman shall hold a clergyman in service but the clerk shall serve him whose seal he bears upon his forehead with heart and mind, being instructed in the things taught him by his bishop. It is hateful and wrong for a clerk to be seen at games or to spend his time hunting or hawking and then, defiled by such sports and full of evil rather than good, to perform the functions of bishop or priest or any other priestly office. For it is written: "Ye who love the Lord hate evil."

We urge upon you also as Christian men that, following the sacred canons, no priest coming from elsewhere be received in the churches founded by you unless he be consecrated by the bishop of your own church or is accepted by him upon letters of recommendation. Some of these deceive themselves; often they are escaped bondsmen, who have declared themselves to their masters as ordained priests but are really servants of the devil, not of God, as are those likewise who receive them; for it is written, "When thou sawest a thief, thou consentedst with him." Let no one of you, therefore, beloved, admit a priest into any church without consulting first his bishop and unless his record and his character have been approved by your bishop.

As to monasteries built by you or erected by the devotion of the faithful: it is ordered that if a monk or a nun, who happens to be a member of the founder's family, be set to preside there, whether as abbot or as abbess, he or she shall be consecrated by the bishop of the city. And when the monastic community has been established there, if after the death of the abbot or abbess a successor is chosen by the community, he or she is nevertheless to be consecrated by the bishop and not inducted by the founder of the cloister; for what has once been offered to God should remain fixed and inviolate under the rule of the bishop. It is ordered also that the consecrated abbott or abbess should first be taught in the whole divine law and in Holy Scripture, so that having learned how to obey they may afterward know how to rule with moderation.

The distribution of tithes of the faithful offered in churches is not to be under control of the giver, for the ordinances of the holy fathers provide that the bishop is to divide them into four parts. How can he who, having put his hand to the plow by God's command, looks backward, be fit to enter the kingdom of God? It is established that the disposition of church funds shall be in the hands of the bishop together with his attendant clergy. It is written: "They which wait upon the altar shall have their portion with the altar." Out of these revenues provision shall be made for alms to the poor, the building of churches, the equipment of altars, and the decoration of every church, according to the income.

A priest or a deacon is on no account to be ordained until his record and his character have been fully investigated. If he is found worthy, let him be ordained by the bishop as above provided. An unfit person or one of servile birth may under no circumstances receive priestly orders or be entrusted with the government of a church.

LXVIII [84]. *Theophylactus, archdeacon of the Roman Church conveys to Boniface the pope's approval of his work*   [748]

To the illustrious father and lord, Archbishop Boniface, holder of the spiritual authority,[1] Theophylactus, an unworthy archdeacon of the Holy Apostolic See.

An ancient sage has declared among his wise sayings: "The words of the wise are as thorns and well-driven nails, because they do not merely touch the faults of wrongdoers but pierce them." Wherefore, I am constrained to chant in deep sorrow that song of David: "I have announced and I have spoken; they are more than can be numbered;" and that many believe, but few are led into the number of the elect, as the Lord also declares, "Many are called, but few are chosen."

We, O illustrious and glorious crown of the priesthood, have carried to the angelic ear of my blessed master all the details of the report which you have sent him.[2] In reply to your roseate [*sic*], angelic, and welcome request, my aforesaid thrice-blessed master deigns to inform you that he approves what you have rightly decided in the case of schismatics and heretics and excommunicates and others who have basely strayed from the rule of the true faith, and rejoices that the people of the Franks and Gauls are embracing the way of faith and striving earnestly under your holy leadership and that the nations are prospering, not merely in the West but everywhere. For it is written: "The prayer of the righteous man availeth much." And likewise David says: "Had not Moses, his chosen one, stood before him in the breach to turn away his wrath lest he should destroy them."

We still preserve our former affection for you, though many peoples and seas divide us, as it is written: "Many waters cannot quench love, neither can the floods drown it." A little gift of blessing as a souvenir of our friendship: cinnamon, spice, pepper, and incense in a sealed packet; and we beg you earnestly to accept

---

[1] *fascibus*, in the sense of authority, in this case *highest* since he was a pontifical legate.

[2] This whole sentence is rather obscure in the Latin original as found in the MSS, due to errors or omissions by the copyist.

the little for the great. For it is written: "The King's daughter within the palace is all glorious." And also: "To him that hath shall be given." For whoso hath perfect love is worthy to receive all gifts by the ministration of the Holy Spirit.

We pray Almighty God, creator and judge of all things, to cause the peoples of the West and all their neighbors to prosper forever in the faith of the Holy Catholic and Apostolic See, through the eloquence of your holy preaching.

LXIX [85]. *Archdeacon Theophylactus to Boniface, sending congratulations on his success and recommendation of Archdeacon Lullus* [746–747]

Theophylactus, an unworthy archdeacon of the Holy Apostolic See, to the illustrious father and lord, the benignant Archbishop Boniface, holder of the spiritual authority.

In pleasant fields of fragrant flowers, the rose is ofttimes hedged about with thorns. And so, under the illumination of the Holy Spirit, the teacher, like the rose, abounding in the honey-sweet doctrine of eternal salvation, blossoms forth wondrously, O thou blessed one, in the fields of Heaven. The talents entrusted to your excelling blessedness will be returned to Christ among the stars, not with a double, but with a sixfold, increase, and the mysterious voice of Christ will be heard in song: "Well done, good and faithful servant! Thou hast been faithful over a few things, I will make thee ruler over many things: enter thou into the joy of thy lord."

We, together with the apostolic and angelic father of our Holy Church Universal, priests, and people, earnestly beseech the favor of the Lord our God for the increase of your work. May He strengthen and preserve those who are enlightened by your teaching, most holy father, and who have drunk from the water of life, and keep them in the way of the holy and orthodox faith. May He cause the hearts of believers to be opened, the veil of darkness to be lifted, and may they, inspired by the Holy Spirit, hasten with joyful courage to the faith of Christ, as the mercy of the Lord has commanded, saying: "I have other sheep, which are not of this fold," et cetera.

And so, master and most holy father, we beg your ambrosial goodness, blessed of God, to receive our beloved Lullus, your blessed archdeacon and our dearest and sweetest companion and brother, with courteous favor for the sake of God and the friendship of our humble self. Our affection for him is based upon his faithful and agreeable services to you, gentle father adorned with many badges of honor. Wherefore, we beg your well-tried prudence on bended knee to grant him a still greater recompense and for the sake of our humble self to remember him whenever you lift your prayers to God, as it is written: "The prayer of the righteous man availeth much."

With these preliminaries we greet your most holy, nectar-sweet divine fatherliness and pray that with God's favor you may receive your eternal reward and may win the desired verdict as your welfare may require.

We are sending you a little gift of spices, cinnamon, and storax (*serostyracem*), as largesse from the blessed Apostle Peter and beg you graciously to accept it.[1]

LXX [86]. *Boniface reports to Pope Zacharias the foundation of the monastery at Fulda* [751]

To the most reverend and beloved lord and master to be revered in fear and honor, Zacharias, endowed with the privilege of the apostolic office and raised to the dignity of the Apostolic See, Boniface, your humble and most unworthy servant, but your most devoted legate in Germany, sends hearty greetings of unfailing love.

I beseech your fatherly and gracious Highness with earnest prayer that you will kindly and favorably receive this priest of mine and bearer of my letter, by name Lullus. He brings certain confidential messages for your gracious hearing only, partly by

---

[1] Making every allowance for obvious defects in the text, the sense both of this and of the previous letter is difficult to reproduce. The flowery extravagance of the style compares most unfavorably with the simplicity of Boniface and may be due to the probable Greek or Syrian origin of the Roman archdeacon.

word of mouth, partly in writing. He will also make certain inquiries of importance to me and bring me the answers and the advice of your fatherly kindness for the comfort of my old age under authority of St. Peter, prince of the Apostles. When you have heard and considered all these matters, if they meet with your approval I shall strive with God's help to enlarge upon them; but if, as I fear, they may not altogether please you I shall follow your apostolic precept and either crave your indulgence or do penance as is fitting.

Your second predecessor, Gregory [II] of reverend memory, when he ordained me—unworthy as I was—and sent me to preach the word of faith to the Germans, bound me by an oath to be the aid and supporter of regular and right-minded bishops and priests in word and deed, and this, by divine grace, I have tried to do. False priests, however, hypocrites, misleading the people, I would either restore to the way of salvation or reject and refrain from communion with them; this I have in part accomplished but in part have not been able to maintain and carry through. In spirit I have kept my vow, because my soul has not consented to their counsels. But in the body I have not been able absolutely to keep apart from them when I have gone to the Frankish court on business of the Church and have found there persons of whom I could not approve. Nevertheless, I have not partaken with them in the holy communion of the body of Christ.

The same apostolic pontiff required me also to report to the pontiff of the Apostolic See upon the customs and way of life of the peoples whom I visited, and I trust in God that I have done this.

In regard to the question of the archbishops and the palliums to be requested from the Roman Church according to the promise of the Franks which I called to the attention of Your Holiness some time since: I have to ask the indulgence of the Apostolic See because after long delay they [the Frankish princes] have not fulfilled their promises, the affair is still being discussed and postponed, and no one knows what they may be willing to do. If it had depended upon me, the promise would have been kept.

There is a wooded place in the midst of a vast wilderness and at the center of the peoples to whom we are preaching. There we have placed a group of monks living under the rule of St. Benedict, who are building a monastery. They are men of strict abstinence, who abstain from meat and wine and spirits, keeping no servants, but content with the labor of their own hands. This place I have acquired by honorable effort, through the help of pious and God-fearing men, especially of Karlmann, formerly prince of the Franks, and have dedicated it in honor of the Holy Savior. Here I am proposing, with your kind permission, to rest my age-worn body for a little time and after my death to be buried here. The four peoples to whom we have spoken the word of Christ by the grace of God dwell, as is well known, round about this place, and as long as I live and retain my faculties, I can be useful to them with your support. It is my desire, upheld by your prayers and led by God's grace, to continue my close relations with you, to remain in your service among the German people to whom I was sent, and to follow your directions, as it is written: "Beloved sons, hear the judgments of your father, and so do that you may be saved." And elsewhere: "He who honors his father lengthens his life." And again: "Honor thy father, that blessing from God may be upon you, and the blessing of the father shall strengthen the house of the sons." . . .[1]

LXXI [87]. *Pope Zacharias replies to the inquiries of Boniface*

Nov. 4, 751

Zacharias, bishop and servant of the servants of God, to Boniface, his most reverend and holy brother and fellow bishop.

May the blessed God, father of our Lord Jesus Christ, who gathers what is scattered and preserves what is gathered, increase the faith and confidence of his own servants in preaching the Gospel of Jesus Christ our Lord, who lives forever in unity with the Father and the Holy Spirit. To Him be glory and praise who is the helper and guardian of those who believe in Him; for He, Himself, has said: "He who believeth in me shall live and not

[1] The letter ends abruptly here, the remainder being lost.

die; for I am the way, the truth and the life." We praise and
exalt His holy name, learning from the bearers of these presents
and from your letters, my brother, that you still live and are strong
in the Lord, and we beseech the unmeasured divinity of our God
that He may long preserve you to preach, even more widely, the
Holy Gospel and the sacrament of His holy faith, may fortify you
with His protection, and guard you against the snares of your
enemies with His tender mercy.

Your Holiness states in your letter that our predecessor, Gregory [II] of blessed memory, pontiff of this Apostolic See, when he
sent you into Germany and to the pagans there received a promise
from you, that so far as you could find orthodox bishops and
priests and such as were perfect in the words of exhortation you
would give them your support and would hold communication
with them, and this you have done. But if you found bishops who
were false guides or priests not truly such, or those who had
strayed from the straight way, you would have no dealings at all
with them. This also you declare you have observed in spirit up
to now, with God's blessing. But if, to secure the favor of the
princes and people of the Franks in behalf of the needs of the
churches of God, you could not escape from personal contact with
them, while at the same time your soul was not infected by their
opinions or by any consent to communion with them, then the fact
of your dealing with them without consenting to their iniquities is
no reproach to you in the sight of God. For if they listen to your
preaching they shall be saved; but if they persist in their wickedness, you will have saved your soul, according to the word of the
prophet.

Concerning the bishops of the Franks and the palliums, you say
that the [princes] have not yet kept their promises. If they do so
according to their word, they will be worthy of praise; but if not,
let them take the consequences. We, by God's grace, give freely
what we have freely received, and as far as you are concerned in
this matter, your good will has been appreciated by us.

You have petitioned that the monastery founded and established
by you in a vast wilderness and dedicated to our God and Savior,
where you have settled monks living under the rule of St. Benedict,

may be granted a privilege in your name by the Apostolic See. This we have ordained in accordance with your wish and petition. It is fitting that the desire of our greatest preacher of the divine ministry should be fulfilled, as it is written in the Lord's word: "He that endureth to the end, the same shall be saved." Also, "Blessed is that servant, whom his lord when he cometh shall find so doing; he will set him over all that he hath."

Your above-mentioned messenger Lullus and his companions have set forth very clearly, in part orally, partly in writing, everything which your Holiness had entrusted to them. To this we have sent replies to you, my brother, also by word of mouth and in writing. In the petition presented by them were the following items about which you inquired of us, which were to be accepted and which rejected.

First as to birds—jackdaws, crows, and storks: these are absolutely forbidden as food for Christians. Beavers, hares, and wild horses are still more strictly prohibited. However, most holy brother, you are well versed in all the sacred writings.

In regard to the Easter fire: the ancient holy fathers prescribe that since the Church of Christ was founded upon His precious blood by the grace of our Lord God, on the fifth day of Easter week, while the sacred oil is being consecrated, three large lamps with oil collected from the various receptacles of the church shall be burned continuously in a remote chamber of the church, symbolizing the inner part of the tabernacle, and carefully tended so that the oil shall suffice for three days. On Holy Saturday fire shall be taken from these lamps for the consecration of the sacred baptismal water and shall be renewed by the priest.

In regard to crystals we have, as you say, no tradition.

You ask what is to be done in the case of men or horses afflicted with leprosy (*morbus regius*). If men are subject to this disease from birth or through inheritance they are to be taken out of the city, but they may be permitted to receive alms from the people. If, however, a person of high or low estate is stricken by the disease not from his birth but in consequence of an illness, he is not to be cast out but is to be cured if possible. But if he comes to a church for Holy Communion he may not be admitted to partake until all the rest have been served. Horses infected with this disease, if they are incurable, are to be thrown into holes or pits, so that others may not be infected by contact with them. Animals torn by mad wolves or dogs are to be kept apart lest they go mad and infect others by their bites, and if there are only a few of them they are to be buried in a pit as I have described.

You inquire whether nuns are to wash each other's feet, as men do, on Holy Thursday as well as on other days. It is the Lord's teaching that he who does good works by faith shall receive praise. Men and women have one God, who is in heaven.

The forms of blessing used by the Gauls vary, as you, my brother, know, with many corruptions. For they do not follow the apostolic tradition but act through vainglory, thus bringing their own damnation; for it is written: "If any man preacheth unto you any gospel other than that which ye have received, let him be anathema." You, beloved brother, have received the rule of the catholic tradition; preach therefore to all and teach all as you have received from the Holy Roman Church, whose servant we are by the will of God.

You ask whether a man may be ordained priest before his thirtieth year. It is well and fitting, beloved, that men of mature years and of good report should be ordained priests according to the sacred canons, if such can be found. But if not, and the need is urgent, let men of twenty-five and upward be ordained priests and deacons, as is provided in the law of God.

As to Milo[1] and his like, who are doing great injury to the Church of God, preach in season and out of season, according to the word of the Apostle, that they cease from their evil ways. If they listen to your admonitions they will save their souls, but if they die in their sins you who preach righteousness shall not lose your reward.

You ask after how long a time bacon fat may be eaten. On this point we have no tradition from the fathers; but since you ask, we advise that it be not eaten until it has been smoked or cooked over a fire. If, however, one prefers to eat it raw this should not be done until after Easter.

[1] Bishop of Trier and Rheims.

That bishop about whom you inquire, who has been convicted of fighting and fleshly lust and after his degradation is still trying to get possession of church property, is to be utterly and shamefully rejected. For what portion has an infidel with the faithful? And what has Christ in common with Belial? These people have been condemned by the tradition of the holy fathers and the ordinances of the sacred canons.

You inquire whether you are in any way to blame for ordaining priests or deacons, who came to you at irregular times with their request, under pressure of necessity or poverty. Our answer is this, my brother: you know well that the sacred canons prescribe the proper times for the ordination of priests. Nevertheless, since you have acted from devotion to the faith we will ask the indulgence of the Lord our God.

As to the church tax of one *solidus* from each manse[1] take it without any hesitation, because from this you can give alms to the needy and maintain the upkeep of the sacred churches, as the canons prescribe.

Priests who were raised from laymen and who had previously a criminal record, which they concealed but whose sin was later discovered, are to be stripped of their priestly dress and placed under penance. For God hates not the repentant sinner but him who denies his sin.

You beg for advice as to whether it is permitted to flee from the persecution of the heathen or not. We give you this wholesome counsel: so long as it can be done, and you can find a suitable place, carry on your preaching; but if you cannot endure their assaults you have the Lord's authority to go into another city.

You ask what is to be done with an excommunicated bishop who pays no attention to the apostolic authority. Such a one is accursed before God and man, and he who is not condemned shall have no part in his condemnation. For they shall be condemned in the day of wrath and the revealing of our Savior Jesus Christ when He shall sit in judgment upon the human race, as it is written: "I will resist the proud, saith the Lord."

You inquire, my brother, whether it is right to take rent from

---

[1] *casata:* apparently the holding of a peasant.

Slavs living on Christian land. On this point you need no advice, for the case is perfectly clear. If they settle without paying tribute they will at some time claim the land as their own; if, on the contrary, they pay tribute, then they will understand that the land has an owner.

You ask us, most holy brother, to inform Your Holiness where the sign of the cross should be made during the recitation of the holy canon. In compliance with your request we have marked in the roll which we have given to your pious priest Lullus the places where the sign of the cross is to be made.

Having thus made all these matters clear, we pray the mercy of God—sinner though we be—to strengthen and comfort you with his aid and to give us the joy of hearing good tidings of your continued well-being.

May God preserve you in safety, most reverend brother.

Given on the eve of the Nones of November in the thirty-second year of our most pious and august Lord Constantine emperor crowned by God, in the eleventh year of his consulship, in the fifth indiction.

LXXII [88]. *Elevation of Mainz to an archbishopric*[1] Nov. 4, 751

Pope Zacharias to Boniface, bishop of the holy church of Mainz and through him [to his successors] in the same venerable church, greeting forever.

How greatly the Lord our God has favored you and worked with you, most holy brother, would take too long to tell, and so

---

[1] Although this letter is included in the correspondence of Boniface, it is obviously spurious. As Tangl in his edition points out, it could not have been issued by Pope Zacharias. Evidence indicates that Mainz was raised to an archbishopric about 780. There appears to be no good explanation for this letter. Probably as good a guess as any is that of Hauck and Tangl to the effect that this may be a reworking of a bull authorizing the elevation of Cologne to an archbishopric. Cf. XLVIII, above; Tangl, *Die Briefe des heiligen Bonifatius*, pp. 198 f. (*Geschichtschreiber der deutschen Vorzeit*, No. 92); and Hauck, *Kirchengeschichte Deutschlands*, I, 562.

what we offer here is only to confirm what we have learned in part from your own narration.

When, therefore, Your Holiness had been sent by our predecessor Gregory [II] of holy memory and after your work had been begun and in part spiritually accomplished, you returned to Rome and were ordained bishop by him and sent back to your mission of preaching. There you have been laboring by God's providence now these five and twenty years in that same preaching since you received the bishopric. In the province of the Franks you held a synod in our stead and in accordance with the canonical rules, and by God's help all were brought to obedience. But while you have been occupied with this holy work you have until now claimed no episcopal see. But now, since God has so widely extended your mission, it becomes our duty to assign to you and your successors a cathedral church in accordance with the petition of the sons of the Franks. Wherefore, by authority of the blessed apostle Peter, we decree that the above-mentioned church of Mainz be established as a metropolitan see to you and your successors forever. It shall have under it these five cities, to wit, Tongres, Cologne, Worms, Speyer, and Utrecht, and all those peoples in Germany to whom your preaching has brought the knowledge of the light of Christ. And, this being now established, we command that the charter of this our confirmation be preserved in your church forever, as evidence thereof.

Farewell.

Given on the eve of the Nones of November in the thirty-second year of our most pious and august Lord Constantine emperor crowned by God, in the eleventh year of his consulship, in the fifth indiction.

LXXIII [89]. *Papal charter for the monastery of Fulda*

[Nov., 751]

Pope Zacharias to Bishop Boniface, and through him to the abbots of the monastery built by him, in succession forever.

Since reasonable requests ought always to be granted, it is right that the devotion of the founder of a pious house of prayers should be acknowledged by the grant of privileges. Wherefore, since you have asked that the monastery of our Savior, built by you in the place called *Bochonia* on the bank of the river Fulda, be given the honor of a privilege from the Apostolic See—so that, being established under the jurisdiction of our Holy Church whose servant we are by God's will, it may not be subject to the control of any other church—we therefore comply with your pious wish and by our authority we effect what you have requested. We forbid by this our authority any priest of any church except the Apostolic See to have any rights whatsoever in the aforesaid monastery, so that no one shall presume, except by invitation of the abbot, even to celebrate Mass there, and so that the monastery shall firmly and forever be endowed with all rights implied in the apostolic privilege.[1]

We give order by this our decree forbidding absolutely all prelates of any church whatsoever and of any rank or invested with any official powers, under penalty of anathema, ever to dare to violate in any way the privilege granted by us to the aforesaid monastery.

Farewell.

LXXIV [90]. *Cardinal-Bishop Benedict to Boniface* [Nov., 751]

To our most holy and best beloved father in Christ, Archbishop Boniface, greeting from Benedict, bishop and vicar of the Holy Apostolic See.

The venerable priest Lullus, here present as messenger of Your Paternal Holiness, has delivered to us your revered communications. The text thereof recites your grievous suffering and distress from men having no fear of God, false bishops, pseudo-priests, lustful clerks, and their evil acts and wicked conduct, as well as from the pressure of hostile peoples. That pressure must end in their everlasting destruction. What sufferings, most holy father,

---

[1] In a much later form of this document the following is here interpolated: "And let the monastery enjoy the property, both real and personal, which it now possesses, as well as whatever divine mercy may be pleased to convey to it in future by the gifts and offerings and tithes of the faithful, free of all control, in perpetual security."

have all the saints endured to win the sure reward of eternal life! We have for our comforter that noble Apostle Paul, who says: "Through much tribulation we must enter into the kingdom of God."

Great shall be your reward, most holy father, and a crown of glory before Almighty God for your endurance of all things for the sake of the divine command and for the preaching of the Gospel of Jesus Christ our Lord God and Savior. Sinner that I am, I beseech His power that, through the intercession of my blessed master Peter, prince of the Apostles, whose vicar you are among wild and savage peoples, He may protect you with His mercy and that, when your ministry is accomplished, you may in the day of the Lord's coming present the abundant fruits of your labor and receive from God, the creator of all things, a hundred-fold reward and may inherit eternal life.

Commending myself also to your holy prayers, I have given your messenger all the help I could in word and deed. The gift sent me by Your Holiness I have received as from a father and have given thanks to Almighty God and to Your Fatherly Holiness.

I am sending you, holy father, a trifling gift, a bath towel (*sabanum*), a face towel (*facitergium*), and a little frankincense, and I beg Your Revered Paternity to accept it without offense.

Farewell in Christ, beloved father.

LXXV [91]. *Boniface begs Archbishop Egbert of York to send him certain works of Bede and inquires regarding procedure against immoral priests* [747–751]

To his friend in the embrace of loving arms, his brother in the bonds of spiritual brotherhood, Archbishop Egbert, clothed with the garment of supreme prelacy, abundant greeting of unfailing love in Christ from Boniface, a humble bishop, legate in Germany of the Roman Catholic and Apostolic Church.

We have received with joyful and grateful heart the gifts and the books sent us by you. With hands upraised to heaven we have besought the Majesty Supreme to bestow on you abundant rewards in the highest sphere of the angels. But now we beg the clemency of Your Holiness, with earnest prayer, that your affection may deign to pray for us in our struggles and trials. The great burden upon us compels us to seek the aid of righteous men, as it is written: "The earnest prayer of the righteous man availeth much." The brevity of a letter, however, prevents us from telling all the ills we suffer both within and without.

Now we exhort you with eager desire to comfort our sorrow, as you have done before, by sending us some spark from that light of the Church which the Holy Spirit has kindled in your land: namely, that you will be so kind as to send us some portion of the treatises which Bede, that inspired priest and student of the Sacred Scriptures, has put forth in his writings. Most especially, if possible, his lectionary for the year [the homilies], which would form a convenient and useful manual for us in our preaching, and the Proverbs of Solomon. We hear that he has written commentaries on this book.

Meantime we greatly need your advice and counsel. When I find a priest who long since fell into carnal sin and after doing penance was restored to his office by the Franks, and now, dwelling in a large district with no other priests, is administering baptism and celebrating Mass for a population who are believers but are prone to error; if now I withdraw him, according to the most approved canons, then, on account of the scarcity of priests, infants will die without the sacred water of rebirth unless I have some better man to replace the former one. Judge therefore between me and the erring people, whether it is better, or at least the lesser evil, that such a man should perform the service of the sacred altar or that the mass of the people should die as pagans because they have no way of securing a better minister. Or if, in the multitude of priests, I find one who has fallen into that same sin and has been reinstated in his former rank through penitence, so that the whole body of priests and people have confidence in his good character, and if he should now be degraded, his secret sin would be revealed, the mass of the people would be shocked, many souls would be lost through the scandal, and there would be great hatred against priests and distrust in the ministers of the Church, so that they would all be despised as faithless and unbelieving. Therefore we have boldly ventured to bear with this man and allow him to remain in the sacred ministry, thinking the danger from the offense of one man would be less evil than the perdition of the souls of almost the entire people. On this whole subject I earnestly desire your holy advice in writing, as to how much I should bear to avoid scandal and how much I should repress.

Finally, we are sending you by the bearer of this letter two small casks of wine, asking you, in token of our mutual affection, to use it for a merry day with the brethren. We beg that you will so treat our requests that your reward may shine forth in the highest heavens.

LXXVI [93]. *Boniface asks for the support of Abbot Fulrad of St. Denis in his petition to King Pippin in behalf of his Anglo-Saxon associates—also for the appointment of Lullus as his successor* [752?]

Boniface, servant of the servants of God and bishop by the grace of Christ, to his best-beloved fellow ecclesiastic Fulrad, priest, perpetual greeting of love in Christ.

I know not how to return such thanks as you deserve for the spiritual friendship which you for God's sake have so often shown to me in my troubles, but I pray the Almighty to reward you forever in the highest heavens and in the joy of the angels. And now I pray that you may carry through to the end the good work you have so well begun; namely, that you will salute our glorious and gracious King Pippin from me and will convey my deepest gratitude to him for all the kindness he has shown me and will report to him what my friends and I feel as to the future. It seems to us that on account of my infirmities I must soon end this mortal life and the daily course of my activities. Wherefore I pray His Royal Highness in the name of Christ, the Son of God, to indicate to me while I am still living what provision he may be willing to make thereafter in regard to my disciples. They are nearly all foreigners. Some are priests living in many places in the service of the Church and of the people. Some are monks in our cloisters or are children learning to read. Others are mature men who have long been living with me and helping in my work. I am anxious about all these, that after my death they may not face dispersion but may have the support and patronage of Your Highness[1] and not be scattered abroad like sheep without a shepherd—also that those peoples which are near the pagan border may not lose the law of Christ.

For this reason, I earnestly beseech your gracious favor in God's name to cause my son the auxiliary bishop Lullus to be appointed to this [my] ministry to the people and the churches, as preacher and teacher for priests and people, if it please God and Your Grace. And I hope, God willing, that the priests may have in him a master, the monks a teacher according to the rule, and the Christian people a faithful preacher and pastor. I make this request especially because my priests living near the border of the heathen lead a very meagre existence. They can get enough to eat but cannot procure clothing without help and protection from elsewhere, as I have assisted them to maintain themselves in those regions for the service of the people.

And if the grace of Christ shall move you to consent to my requests, kindly send word to me by these present messengers or in writing, so that I may live or die more happily in the security of your care.

LXXVII [94]. *A letter of consolation from Boniface to the Abbess Bugga*   [732–754]

To his venerable and much beloved sister, Bugga, Boniface called also Winfred sends heartfelt greetings in the love of Christ.

Since we have so long been separated, beloved sister, through the fear of Christ and my love of wandering, by a wide space of

---

[1] This letter, while it is addressed to Fulrad, is so obviously intended for the king that former editors have imagined that it was a patchwork of two separate epistles. I see no reason to think that it is anything more than another case of Boniface's frequent habit of shifting his form of address to follow the course of his thought. It was good diplomacy to make use of a powerful churchman to influence the king in his behalf.

land and sea, I have learned from many reports of the storms of
troubles which with God's permission have befallen you in your
old age. I have deeply regretted that after you had thrown off
the pressing cares of monastic rule in your desire for a life of
contemplation, still more insistent and more weighty troubles
have come upon you.

And so now, my revered sister, in sympathy with your misfortunes and mindful of your kindnesses to me and of our ancient
friendship, I am sending you a brotherly letter of comfort and
exhortation. Remember that word of the Truth: "Possess your
souls in patience," and the saying of Solomon the Wise, "Whom
the Lord loveth he chasteneth and every son in whom he delight-
eth." Also the word of the Psalmist, "Many are the afflictions of
the righteous, but the Lord delivereth him out of them all"; and
elsewhere, "The sacrifices of God are a broken spirit; a broken
and a contrite heart, O God, thou wilt not despise." And remember
the saying of the Apostle: "Through much tribulation we must
enter into the kingdom of God." And again: "Let us rejoice in
our tribulations, knowing that tribulation worketh patience; and
patience, probation; and probation, hope; and hope putteth not to
shame."

In that hope, beloved sister, rejoice and be glad always, for
you shall not be put to shame. Scorn earthly trials with your whole
soul; for all soldiers of Christ of either sex have despised temporal
troubles and tempests and have held the frailties of this world as
naught—witness the word of St. Paul: "When I am weak, then
am I strong." And again: "Who shall separate us from the
love of Christ? shall tribulation?" and so forth to "him that loved
us." The same Father and lover of your virgin purity who called
you to Himself with the voice of fatherly love in your early youth,
saying in the words of the Prophet: "Hearken, O daughter, and
consider and incline thine ear; forget also thine own people and
thy father's house; for the king has desired thy beauty," He it is
who now, in your old age desires to adorn the beauty of your soul
with labor and sorrow.

Do you then, beloved, rejoicing in the hope of a heavenly fatherland, hold the shield of faith and patience against all adversity of mind or body. With the help of your bridegroom Christ carry through in your beautiful old age to the glory of God the building of that Gospel tower begun in your early youth, so that at the coming of Christ you may be found worthy to meet Him among the wise virgins, bearing a lamp with the oil burning.

Meanwhile I pray earnestly that you will remember your ancient promise to pray for me that the Lord, who is the Redeemer and Savior of us all, may rescue my soul from its manifold perils to my spiritual advantage.

Farewell in Christ.

LXXVIII [95]. *Boniface commends a messenger to Count Reginbert* [732-754]

To his dear son Count Reginbert, Boniface, servant of the servants of God, sends greeting without end in the Lord.

We beg the favor of your high office, that you may be pleased to allow this bearer of my letters, on his way to Rome to offer prayers and bring replies in church matters, to pass safely through your territory and assist him when in need, as you have done by former messengers of ours according to their reports when they have returned.

Pray comply with this request that your reward before God may be increased and multiplied.

Farewell in Christ.

LXXIX [96]. *Boniface to Lioba, abbess of Bischofsheim*
[735-754]

To the reverend handmaid of Christ, Lioba, held ever in sincere affection, Boniface, servant of the servants of God, sends heartfelt greeting in Christ.

Be it known to you, dear and holy sister, that our brother and fellow priest Torthat has reported to us that in response to his request you are willing to permit a certain maiden to receive instruction for a time, if we would give our consent. Be assured, therefore, that whatever you may see fit to do in this matter for the increase of her merits shall have our consent and approval.

Farewell in Christ.

LXXX [97]. *Cena*[1] *asks the friendly interest of Boniface*
[723–754]

To the venerable pontiff, Boniface, lover of Christ, Cena the unworthy sends greeting.

I must confess to you, dearest friend, that although my bodily eyes see you but seldom, I never cease to look upon you with the eyes of the spirit. These little gifts are tokens of affection, but are quite unworthy of Your Holiness. Please believe that so long as I live I shall always remember you in my prayers. I beg you by our trusted friendship to be loyal to my insignificance, as I have faith in you, and to aid me with your prayers so that Almighty God may order my life according to His will.

If any of your people should ever come to this country, I beg him to inform me, and if I can be of service in any way by supplying bodily comforts or spiritual support to you or any of yours, pray let me know. I am sure that it will greatly help toward the salvation of my soul, if I follow your commands with my whole strength.

Farewell in the Lord.

LXXXI [99]. *Boniface commends a serf to the priest Denehard*
[732–754]

Boniface, servant of the servants of God, to the priest Denehard, greeting in Christ.

I commend to you, dear friend, this serf Athalere, begging you to aid him in case of need as if he were a free man and to pledge

---

[1] The personality of the writer is quite obscure. She may have been abbess of a convent somewhere in Frankland.

yourself to his friends for him as such and not as for a serf. Since he is proposing to take a wife, I am thus eager to commend him, that he may have no fears on account of his servile condition.

Farewell in Christ.

LXXXII [101]. *The priest Wigbert writes to the monks of Glastonbury an account of his arrival in Germany and his reception by Boniface*   [732–754]

To my holy masters loved in Christ, fathers and brothers dwelling in the Abbey of Glastonbury, the priest Wigbert, humble servant of you and of the servants of God, greeting in the Lord.

The blessed God, "who desires all men to be saved and to come to a knowledge of the truth," has been pleased to guide our way in safety into these lands, that is, into the borders of the pagan Hessians and Saxons, across the sea and amid the perils of this world, through no merit of our own, but by your permission and prayers and by His own mercy. You know, my brethren, that the wide spaces of the earth cannot separate us who are bound together in the love of Christ. The reverent kinship I bear to you and my prayers to God in your behalf are always present with me.

I want you to know, beloved, that our Archbishop Boniface when he heard of our arrival had the kindness to come a long way to meet us and gave us a gracious welcome. And believe me that our labor is not in vain in the Lord, but shall bring a reward to you. For Almighty God in his mercy and through your merits has given success to our labors, arduous and perilous though they be in almost every way, hunger and thirst and cold and attacks by the heathen. So I beg you to pray for us "that utterance may be given unto me in opening my mouth" and that the fruits of our work may be permanent.

Farewell in the Lord. Salute the brethren round about—first Abbot Ingeld and our own community. Carry to our mother Tetta and to those who are with her the news of our successful journey. I beg you all to repay our instant prayers in your behalf, and may divine mercy keep Your Holiness ever in prayer for us.

LXXXIII [103]. (*Lullus*)[1] *asks permission of Boniface to remain in Thuringia for purposes of study* [c. 739–741]

To my best beloved teacher, most diligent in the pursuit of learning, Archbishop Boniface, wearing the insignia of the supreme pontificate, I, N., being one among many, send a greeting of devoted love in Christ as a slight acknowledgment of your kindness to me.

The Holy Scripture admonishes us to do nothing hastily and without reflection, as it is written: "Do all things cautiously," etc., Wherefore I have thought best to send a letter in my crude style to Your Lofty Wisdom and to state the occasion of my request—nay, of my desire to make a request—so that, looking at it from every side, my cautious adviser may decide as may seem best to him and indicate to me, his servant, his decision, which I shall gladly and humbly accept.

I confess to you, dearest of masters, that since I came to Thuringia by permission of Your Holiness, for the purpose of study and investigation—for, if my tiny spark of intelligence is able to learn or inquire into anything I owe it, under God, to your kindness— I have not been able to apply myself to study as closely as I knew I ought to do. This was due to two causes, a dimness of eyesight and headaches, and especially to a third, trouble of the intestines causing a dullness of the mind. Will your fatherly kindness, therefore, permit me to remain a little longer, so that you, who, according to the Apostle, have fed with milk your thirsty child not yet able to take solid food, may in due time receive him back into your service with health restored through the favoring grace of Christ and the intercession of your prayers. But if your judgment shall decide otherwise, then, if He to whom endless ages have added nothing and from whom they have taken nothing away shall give me strength, I will return at such time as you direct.

Meanwhile, by the mercy of God which fills the whole earth I beseech you, as it were on bended knees, embracing the feet of Your Highness in supplication, that you may be pleased to intercede before the merciful and righteous Judge for my count-

---

[1] The authorship of this letter is uncertain, but all the circumstances point to Lullus, and the pompous, affected style confirms the supposition.

less sins and transgressions. Yet may I not disturb the serenity of Your Grace; for our Jesus, glory of heaven and Savior of the world, to whom all things are known and from whom no secrets are hid, commands us saying: "Ask and ye shall receive," etc.

Nor do I expect that a whirlwind can be found to rescue me from this distress, but rather some remedy for my health, knowing myself to be a sick man and seeking for a physician.

The little verses below I send to you, my dear father, for correction, hoping that you will be kind enough to send me your comments, that I may clearly understand my own errors.

May the Holy and Indivisible Trinity preserve Your Eminence to preside over the people of the churches far and wide so long as you live and to overcome all the assaults of your enemies.

May God Almighty steadily increase your wealth in active mercy by granting you the gain of many souls, until you may, finally rich in heavenly possessions, receive your recompense, which is the joyful voice of God calling out to you: "My good and trusted servant! Now, do thou rise to the highest joys of God, thy Lord, which are thine also. Because thou wert trustworthy when thou hadst few, I will raise thee over many." Thus a rest that cannot fail you, salvation, and the fulfillment of your hopes shall come to you, with the help of God—of God who created all things at once, who lives and rules, one and the same, before all time and without beginning or end. Whose bountiful mercy admonished me in wretchedness to come to you as to a master, at a time when, bereft of inner light, crushed by the heavy burden of sin, I was pursuing sloth, which ever proveth deadly to the souls of all men but which I believed to be a source of happiness. Grace, however, descending from Christ, my Savior, dispelled the darkness from my dull spirit and mercifully blessed my stunted senses with gifts which I had not deserved. For Him unending Glory and Honor! But for you, may a Crown, a reward both of your labor and of that great talent of which I am but the slightest particle, grow on the Heights of Paradise, for you have been a Guide on the straight path which leads thereto.[1]

---

[1] In the translation of this passage it seemed unwise to attempt to retain the verse form of the original.

LXXXIV [104]. *Boniface to Cardinal-Deacon Gemmulus*
[742-754]

To his most reverend and beloved son, Archdeacon Gemmulus, Boniface, a humble servant of the servants of God, sends affectionate greetings of eternal love.

It often happens that love unites in spirit those who are widely separated in the body. And this is one of the most familiar sorrows of the traveler, that he has to think of his far distant friend with grief and sadness while he himself is suffering annoyance and persecution from an enemy near at hand. Would that I might have you near, my brother, as the comforter of my wanderings, might use your holy counsel, rejoice in your sympathy, be happy in the sight of your dear face, and be refreshed by your blessed encouragement.

But since the course of our mortal life and our present circumstances do not permit this, may your affection do that one and greatest thing which God grants and prescribes, saying: "This is my commandment, that ye love one another." May each truly love in God the absent one whom he may not have near in the flesh. And as St. Augustine says: "Though one be in the East and the other in the West, they are never separated because of the love which binds them together." Therefore, as James says, "The prayer of faith shall save him that is sick"; and also, "Pray one for another that ye may be healed." Let us pray one for the other that we may be healed and that the grace of God, which has separated us on earth, may bring us together, rejoicing, in the highest heaven.

LXXXV [105]. *King Ethelbert of Kent sends gifts to Boniface and asks for a pair of falcons* [748-754]

To the most holy Archbishop Winfred, called Boniface and worthily adorned with the pontifical insignia, Ethelbert, king of Kent, sends greeting in the Lord of lords.

Some years ago, the venerable abbess Bugga, after a visit to the holy places in the city of Rome for the purpose of offering prayer, returned thence to this, her native land, and to the convent of holy women which she had formerly governed wisely under the law of the Church. At her invitation I had a conference with her in which, among other matters of importance, she called to my especial attention that while you were both at Rome and eagerly engaged in making frequent visits to the shrines of the Holy Apostles, you had given her permission to speak familiarly with Your Gracious and Indulgent Holiness about her own affairs. She further advised me that, impelled by our blood relationship, she had by the earnest solicitation of her prayers obtained from Your Paternity in my behalf the boon that just as she, who was present, received your wholesome precepts and was strengthened by the blessing of your prayers, so I too, though absent and personally unknown to you, through your wonted kindness might be enriched by that same gift, so necessary to me, even as though I had been present. When she told me that you had surely promised to do this, I cannot easily state in words what joy and comfort it brought me. I was so much the more rejoiced—as is wont to happen—because she brought me so precious a gift so suddenly and without expectation.

Wherefore it seems proper and useful that I should address Your Holiness, widely famous as you are, through a friendly letter and by the words of trusty messengers. For this I can imagine no more fitting opportunity than just now when we have here certain clerics of Your Excellence who were sent hither into Britain by you as wise and trustworthy agents and are now anxious, with God's help, to return as soon as possible to your gracious presence. It is, therefore, an especial pleasure to me to send the bearer of this letter, the monk Ethelun, under the protection of the aforementioned men of yours, to deliver into your friendly hands these greetings and requests.

In the first place we declare that all with one accord render abundant thanks to Almighty God who has given you of His grace so plentifully that He has turned a countless multitude of the heathen away from their ancient error of idolatry to the standard of Christian faith through the word and works of your mission. We still pray for greater things with God's help, in the confident hope that He who began the work through you will not fail to carry it on from day to day to even greater results.

By the bearer of this letter I am sending to Your Reverence with my devoted affection a few little gifts: a silver, gold-lined drinking cup (*cancum*) weighing three pounds and a half and two woolen cloaks (*repte*). We are not sending these gifts with the purpose or expectation of receiving any earthly profit or return; but rather on bended knees begging of you what is far more necessary, that in these evil days of manifold and unexpected troubles and in this world so filled with scandals you will deign to aid us with the frequent support of your prayers. And with this same object, may your reverend affection have ever in mind to urge on others so far as you can by command or persuasion, not only so long as you know that I am still in this mortal life, but after my death if you shall survive me.

Having thus briefly mentioned these things, there is one other favor which I desire to ask and which, from all I hear, will not be very difficult for you to grant, namely to send me a pair of falcons of such cleverness and courage that they will without hesitation attack cranes and, having caught them, will bring them to earth. We ask you to procure these birds and send them to us since there are very few hawks of this kind in our country—that is, in Kent—which produce such good offspring, of quick intelligence, combative, and capable of being tamed, trained, and taught for the above-mentioned purpose.

Finally, I pray you to reply to my letter and be so kind as to let me know whether the things I am sending have duly arrived.

May divine grace give Your Holiness long life to pray for us.

LXXXVI [106]. *Boniface asks Optatus, abbot of Monte Cassino to join him in mutual fellowship of prayer*   [750–754]

To his reverend and beloved brother and fellow ecclesiastic, Abbot Optatus, and the whole sacred community cherishing the rule of the regular life under his direction, Boniface, called bishop with no superior merit, sends affectionate greetings of love in Christ.

We earnestly beseech Your Gracious Holiness to receive and hold us, unworthy as we are, in unity of affection and spiritual communion, so that there may be between us one faith in thought and one fidelity in action. . . .[1]

May the light of the Gospel of the glory of Christ and that way of life which we are bound to show to the heathen, walking therein ourselves, not be dimmed or hidden within us. We earnestly pray that there may be between us an intimate tie of brotherly love with common prayer for the living and, for those who have passed from this life, prayers and celebration of Masses, the names of the dead being mutually exchanged.

Meanwhile, if Your Fraternity shall be pleased to command anything for us to do or to say we will comply with your wishes in every way. And may you so act upon our request, that your reward may increase and shine in the highest heavens in the ranks of celestial angels.

May the Savior of the world grant you health and long life with bountiful strength, in the fragrance of the sweetest flowers of word and deed.

LXXXVII [107]. *Boniface to King Pippin* [753]

To the most noble lord, Pippin, king of the Franks, Bishop Boniface sends greeting in the Lord.

We render hearty thanks to Your Gracious Highness and pray the Lord Jesus Christ to grant you eternal reward in the kingdom of heaven, because you have deigned to listen to our petition and so bring comfort to my frail old age. But now, noble son, let me say that I believe, by the mercy of God, I can once more be of service to you, and we therefore ask you to let us know whether we may attend the [coming] assembly to carry out your wishes.

A certain servant of our church, by name Ansfrid, himself an accomplished liar, craftily ran away from us and now comes to us with an order from you that justice be done him. We have sent him back to you with our messenger and a letter, so that you may know that he has lied to you, and beg you, in your own interest, to protect us against such deceivers and not to believe their falsehoods.

[1] Some Biblical quotations are here omitted.

LXXXVIII [108]. *Boniface greets the new pope, Stephen II*
[752]

To the most noble lord, Pope Stephen, exalted and beloved above all pontiffs, endowed with the privilege of the apostolate, Boniface, a humble bishop and disciple of the Roman Church, sends affectionate greeting of love in Christ.

I pray Your Gracious Holiness from the depths of my heart that I may be worthy to claim and to possess that intimate union with the Apostolic See under your gentle sway and to remain your faithful and devoted servant and disciple in the same way that I have already served the Apostolic See under three of your predecessors, the two Gregorys and Zacharias of venerable memory, who always helped and strengthened me with their letters of exhortation and with their authority. I pray Your Grace so to act that I may still more efficiently carry out and fulfill your fatherly intentions. For, if I have accomplished anything of value in this Roman mission in which I have been engaged now these six and thirty years, I desire to increase and fulfill it. Or if it be found that I have said or done anything wrong or unwise I pledge myself to correct it humbly and willingly at once according to the judgment of the Roman Church.

Meanwhile I beg my gracious lord not to be offended by my tardiness in sending letters and a personal messenger to you. This delay was owing to my great preoccupation with the restoration of the churches burned by the heathen. Within our parishes and cloisters they have pillaged and burned more than thirty churches. It was this, not any careless negligence, which delayed my letters and my address to Your Paternity.

LXXXIX [109]. *Boniface to Pope Stephen II concerning the dispute with Cologne about the bishopric of Utrecht*   [753]

To his venerable and beloved apostolic lord, Pope Stephen, Boniface, a humble legate or messenger in Germany of the Catholic and Apostolic Church, sends greetings of love in Christ.

In the time of Sergius [687–701], pontiff of the Apostolic See, there came to the shrine of the Holy Apostles a certain Saxon priest of wondrous holiness and self-denial, by name Willibrord, called also Clemens. The aforesaid pope ordained him bishop and sent him on to preach to the heathen Frisians by the shores of the western sea. For fifty years he preached to the Frisian people, converted a great part of them to the faith of Christ, destroyed their temples and holy places, and built churches, establishing an episcopal see with a church in honor of the Holy Savior in a fortified place called Utrecht. In that see and in the church which he had built he continued preaching up to his feeble old age. He also appointed an auxiliary bishop as his substitute to carry on his ministry and at the close of his long life entered into the peace of God.

Then Karlmann, prince of the Franks, entrusted that see to me to appoint a bishop and consecrate him, and this I did.

But now the bishop of Cologne claims for himself that see of the aforesaid Bishop Clemens, who was ordained by Pope Sergius, and declares that it belongs to him on account of the ruins of a certain little church destroyed by the heathen. This Willibrord discovered, razed to the ground within the fortress of Utrecht, rebuilt from the foundations with his own labor, and consecrated in honor of St. Martin. He insists that the castle of Utrecht, together with the ruined church, was given by Dagobert, formerly king of the Franks, to the diocese of Cologne on condition that the bishop of Cologne should convert the Frisians to the Christian faith and should be their pastor. But this he did not do. He did not preach to the Frisians nor convert them to Christianity. The Frisian people remained pagans until Sergius, reverend pontiff of the Roman See, sent the aforesaid servant of God, Willibrord, as bishop and preacher to them. He, as I have said before, converted them to the faith of Christ.

And now the bishop of Cologne wishes to annex this see of the missionary Willibrord, so that there shall be no episcopal see under the Roman pontiff for the Frisian mission. I answered him according to my conviction, that the order of the Apostolic See, the consecration by Pope Sergius, and the mission of the revered preacher Willibrord ought to be far stronger reasons for the establishment of an episcopal see under the Roman pontiff for the Frisian mission—a great part of them being still pagans—than the broken foundations of a little ruined church which had been trampled upon by pagans and abandoned by the neglect of bishops. He, however, does not agree to this.

So now may Your Paternity be pleased to give judgment for me. If my answer to the bishop of Cologne is right and acceptable to you, confirm it by your authority, so that the degree of Sergius and the see itself may be permanently established. It would be a great help to us if you would be willing to send me from the archives of your church a copy of the written instructions of the holy Sergius to Bishop Willibrord, who was ordained by him, so that by authority of Your Holiness I may be able to convince and overcome my opponents. If, however, some other course seems wiser to Your Holiness, be pleased to send me your advice that I may govern myself accordingly.

XC [111]. *Archbishop Cuthbert of Canterbury to Bishop Lullus on the death of Boniface* [After June 5, 754]

To his very reverend brother and fellow bishop, Lullus, beloved in Christ and also to your fellow workers, bishops and priests of God, whose names are written in the book of life, Cuthbert, servant of the servants of God, together with the other fellow ecclesiastics of Christ, both priests and abbots, sends greetings of eternal peace and welfare.

We declare, beloved, with a mind clear before God and his chosen angels, that when we hear by common report of your love of peace, your increase of prosperity, your progress in the sacred religion of Christ, and the fruits of your holy preaching, we are greatly rejoiced and render thanks in earnest prayer to God, the dispenser of all good. But when any harm comes to your religious life or any injury is inflicted upon you, then grief and sorrow afflict us; for as we rejoice with your joy in Christ, even so do we suffer with you in Christ for your adversity.

We can never forget the anguish of varied and continued suffering which you yourself endured for such a long time in company with our father beloved of God, the martyr Boniface of blessed memory, in the midst of pagan tormentors, heretical and schismatic false leaders, in your pilgrimage so filled with cruel dangers, for love of your eternal home. He with his many intimate companions has entered with joy and glory through the agony of martyrdom into the eternal rest of his heavenly fatherland, while you, the survivor of such men, walk with so much the greater difficulty and danger in the midst of divers trials now that you are for the present deprived of so great a father and teacher.

And, although this bitter sorrow tortures our heart, nevertheless a certain triumphant, exulting joy softens and quiets our grief as we recall the wondrous—nay, the ineffable—grace of God and render thanks that the English people were found worthy, foreigners as they are, to send out this gifted student of heavenly learning, this noble soldier of Christ, with many pupils well taught and trained, to far-off spiritual conflicts and for the salvation of many souls through the grace of Almighty God.

This leader and standard-bearer, going on before and breaking down opposition with the help of God, brought most savage peoples from their long and devious wanderings in the wide abyss of eternal perdition into the glorious pathways of the heavenly fatherland by the inspiration of his holy words and by the example of his pious and gentle life. That this was really accomplished the results show more clearly than words, even in those places into which no teacher had ventured before with the Gospel message. For this reason we hold this man in reverend affection among the greatest and most distinguished teachers of the orthodox faith since that incomparable mystery of the choice of apostles for the whole world and the ministry of the disciples of Christ preaching the Gospel at that time.

Wherefore, in our general synod at which we took counsel together regarding those other matters which we have briefly set forth to Your Holiness, we decided to celebrate annually the day of his martyrdom and of the company who perished with him. We desire him to be our especial patron, together with St. Gregory and St. Augustine, and we surely believe that he is such before Christ our Lord, whom he so loved in his life and so glorified in his death as to be worthy of His grace.

Further, we declare ourselves always ready to help and comfort you with fatherly and brotherly words, whenever and however we can, in your work of supervision—now checked, if I may say so, by the loss of a *pater familias*—and we say the same also for the whole company of the servants of God under your direction. And so, in the first place, in proof of the love we bear to you in the depths of our heart we make use of the words and the thought of the Apostle and say with him: "Grace be unto you and peace; we give thanks to God always for you all, making mention of you in our prayers; remembering without ceasing your work of faith and labor of love, and patience of hope, in our Lord Jesus Christ, in the sight of God and our Father." Already during the life of Boniface, of reverend memory, we established our mutual relations by the exchange of letters and by trusty messengers, and now we think it important to renew them; namely, that we should come as suppliants before the living God with mutual supplications for ourselves and for our people, both the living and the dead, with prayers and Masses according to the apostolic command: "Pray for each other that you may be saved." For thus, as is well known, we may secure the divine mercy for ourselves by offering to Him the pure libation of our prayers. Thus shall we find that same mercy aiding us in adversity. For where the help of God is with us according to his own promises there all the enmity of the wicked is put to flight. He himself has said: "If two of you shall agree on earth as touching any thing that they shall ask, it shall be done for them of my Father which is in heaven."

In our judgment this ought now to be done the more zealously and wisely because, according to the apostolic prediction, "perilous times are before us," and the rest of that same epistle. There is no need for me to remind you of outward misfortunes, such as persecution, plunder, hatreds, and scandals which I understand you have suffered, but behold in how many places the condition of the Christian religion is unstable, and how almost everywhere, both within and without, the order of church affairs is disturbed, while on almost every side pernicious sects arise with evil ways of life. And no wonder, when the decrees of the early fathers are thrown aside and the laws of the Church neglected, while so many are following their own inventions, and having ideas injurious to the welfare of many are publishing these and acting upon them, as in fact was said and done a year ago by a certain man of great authority.

But we, timid, I fear, and none too warm in our zeal for righteousness—what should we first of all do other than call without ceasing upon the aid of the holy apostles and martyrs of Christ and the venerable heads of the churches of God, that the grace of Christ may enable us to persevere with unfailing watchfulness in the work to which we are called and appointed? Let us not be blameworthy, but more acceptable, not slothful but energetic, not dividing but bringing together as many as possible into the unity of the Christian faith and uniformity in the ecclesiastical discipline, so that the ministry of our service and the excellence of our work may redound to the praise and glory of Almighty God and we may be found worthy to hear, among those who serve God acceptably: "Blessed is the servant whom the Lord, when he cometh, shall find watching; Verily I say unto you, that he shall make him ruler over all his goods."

We recall these things to memory, for example, when we think of that noble teacher and martyr Boniface, with what diligence he labored in the knowledge of God, what perils and what trials he bore willingly even unto death for the love of Christ and for the saving of souls. And since he has now joined the household of the Almighty it is the part of wisdom for you carefully to weigh his admonitions and to follow his example with all your strength. For, in so far as he is made the intimate of Him whom he loved more than all else, so much the more can he obtain from Him. But also, if those who were placed under him by divine providence shall now depart from his spiritual instruction or fall into evil ways, then he who might have been their advocate in the final judgment will rather be their accuser and will require of them the more strict account before that judge.

On the other hand, those who diligently live up to the standard of his holy teaching and administration, let them be assured that they shall have perpetual communion with that Roman and Apostolic Church which sent him to them as its legate and teacher and, together with her, perpetual communion with us also, living and dying, in prayers and Masses, as we have said. Provided only that they are willing to obey you, the teachers and guides of their welfare, in humility and love, not disloyal or deceitful, but ever going forward like good disciples, faithful to the leaders of their warfare in Christ, to the prize of the high calling of God and the glory of the heavenly kingdom.

We are sending these words of salutation to Your Holiness, not as to one ignorant or needing the example of our unlearned discourse, but for the sake of our mutual affection and support. We bear witness and pray by Almighty God and His Son Jesus Christ, His coming and His kingdom, that you all, beloved, with all those under your rule, may work together in unity, always helping one another against all enemies of the orthodox faith, heretics, schismatics, and men of evil life. So shall you be loved and praised by all good men, dear and acceptable to God Almighty. And so, together with your blessed father and predecessor, you may be worthy to hear that welcome word from Christ the judge of all: "Well done, thou good and faithful servant! Thou hast been faithful over a few things, I will make thee ruler over many things: enter thou into the joy of thy Lord." Amen.

May Almighty God deign to keep you all safe, beloved brothers and sons, in his holy love and fear.

XCI [112]. *Bishop Milret of Worcester to Lullus on the death of Boniface* [After June 5, 754]

To the most kindly and best beloved master in Christ, Bishop Lullus, Milret, servant of those who serve God.

After I had been obliged to leave your company and the bodily vision of the most holy and blessed father Boniface and had come to the land of my birth, through divers accidents and many adventures with the aid of your gracious prayers, a full year had not passed when the sad news was brought to us that our blessed father had passed from the prison of the flesh to the world above. We may well call this sad news, and yet, when we have been permitted to send such an advocate before us into the kingdom of heaven, we have entire confidence that we are in every way supported by God's help and by his holy intercession. And though we lament with many and bitter tears the comfort we have lost in this present life, yet he who is now consecrated a martyr to Christ by the shedding of his blood, the glory and crown of all those whom the fatherland has sent forth, soothes and relieves our saddened hearts by his blessed life, by the fulfillment of his noble work, and by his glorious end. We mourn our fate, lingering in this vale of tears and in this life filled with temptations. He, his pilgrimage accomplished with mighty effort, has attained to a glorious death as a martyr of Christ and now sits in joy above in the heavenly Jerusalem, to be, as I believe, a faithful intercessor for our transgressions, if God's grace permit, together with Christ and the holy citizens of heaven. So much I write of our most loving father and beg you earnestly to send me an account of his venerable life and his glorious end.

One other thing occurs to me to say in view of our close association, and I humbly beg of your precious affection, as if I were now kneeling at your feet, that you will cherish in your heart not as a passing memory but permanently that brotherly love which our common father, Boniface of blessed and holy memory, impressed upon us with his holy words in the love of Christ, joining us in his gracious utterances. I am sure that it will, beyond all doubt, profit both you and me if we strive to carry out the precepts of so great a teacher.

Do not hesitate, most loving master, to instruct me, the least deserving of all your brethren, in brotherly love, to fortify me with your holy precepts and support me with your gracious prayers. I pledge myself to follow faithfully all your directions willingly and in all things as far as I am able, and I promise, as God is my witness, to maintain that firm friendship as long as the spirit governs these limbs and the breath of life dwells in these mortal members. I pray with all my strength that with Christ's help the Scripture may be fulfilled: "They had all things in common."

All this which I have thus briefly set down I have undertaken to send you verbally and more fully by the bearers of this letter, if Almighty God shall prosper the journey. We have sent you also some little gifts which we beg you to accept in the same affectionate spirit in which they are given.

May Christ be pleased to protect you in your loving intercession for our sins.

The book I am not sending because Bishop Gutbert [of Canterbury] has not yet returned it.

Emmanuel.

XCII [115]. *Description of a vision, written to a monk by an unknown author*[1]   [After 757]

. . . some [souls] up to the armpits or to the neck; and over the heads of others rose a seething whirlpool of fire and blackness. There a multitude of abbots, abbesses, counts, and souls of both sexes were seen in various kinds of torment. Places were prepared for many of those now living, of high and low degree according to what their sins deserved. All the souls in pits were to be set free at some time, either in the day of judgment or before. He told of one woman released from a pit by the celebration of Mass; and this, he said, was the highest good for souls who had left the body. The whole race of men was brought together by souls from the whole world before his sight, so that he was able to discern in that moment whatever of good or evil each one had done while he was in the body and to report the merits of almost all living men.

He declared that he saw there a land of the living and the joyful, filled with fragrant flowers and many souls of men known and

[1] Occurs only in the Vienna manuscript. The first folio was cut out, but the contents may be surmised by comparison with our No. II.

unknown to us. Then he saw, leading from this land up to the first heaven, a pathway in the form of a rainbow, then another to the second and from the second to the third, and groups of men clothed in white, both living and dead, and the higher heaven always more beautiful than the lower. And in the monastery itself at Ingedraga [?], while all remained, he was called upon by the judge to declare all [his] faults and sins; but to others this was neither commanded nor forbidden. He told us a great many details, naming them separately, which it would take long to relate and some of which I cannot remember. But this I do recall: that he saw three troops of enormous demons—one in the air, one on land, and a third on the sea—preparing torments for the places of penitence. He saw the first troop striving to deceive men in this our common life and the second pursuing souls through the air, as they emerged from the prison of the body, and dragging them away to torment.

In the penitential pits were plunged Cuthburga and Wiala, once crowned with queenly power—one, Cuthburga, up to the armpits, her head and shoulders clear, her other members covered with spots. Above the head of the other—that is, Wiala—he saw a flame spreading and burning the whole soul at once. The tormentors themselves threw the carnal sins of these women in their faces like boiling mud, and he heard their horrible howls resounding, as it were, through the whole world.

Here, too, he saw the banished Count Ceolla Snoding, bent backward and his head and feet fastened with hooks; also your abbot in the aforesaid double smoke, and Ethelbald, formerly a royal tyrant, and a great multitude of mourning children who had died without baptism under Bishop Daniel. The form of each one, according to the special likeness of the soul, was the same in the limbs, but the faces were different, some shining with the brightness of the sun, some of the moon, others of the stars.

But as to those who are still living, scorners of so beneficent a revelation, the knight Daniel and Bregulf and their like, their vulgar debaucheries and the punishments due them, I think best not to relate what he declared he had seen.

At the end of his vision he heard an indescribable sound re-echoing above through the threefold regions of celestial lights and the multitudes abiding therein, like the sound of many trumpets coming down to the lower levels, marvelously penetrating. Immediately after this, as the vision faded and while his angelic guides were urging him to remember faithfully his Creator's love, he was returned to his body. But still, in the limits of the flesh he saw for some time a countless multitude of unclean spirits groaning in misery because they knew that their evil deeds were found out by men through a divine dispensation.

In confirmation of this revelation he predicted his recovery from a disease which had spread over almost his entire body for two years, and we now perceive that this has been fulfilled by the mercy of God. Furthermore, he revealed to his intimates specific things unknown to others—and not merely to these, but also to the king and the queen and to bishops and many others whom it would take long to enumerate. He also imposed a fast of forty days for the general offenses of [his] whole family according to the order of the same judge. He predicted that vengeance would come upon men in their own persons on account of their neglect of God's commands in external things and many similar matters. He protested with grief that when he had viewed this wretched life from a loftier level he had seen it covered, as it were with a black garment, by the sins of pride, envy, greed, slander, and others, and left without the light of eternal splendor.

Farewell in Christ, in brotherly love and prayers without ceasing.

Bibliography

Betten, Francis S., St. Boniface and St. Virgil: a Study from the Original Sources of Two Supposed Conflicts . . . Washington, D. C., 1927. "Benedictine Historical Monographs," 2.

Böhmer, Johann F., Regesta zur Geschichte der Mainzer Erzbischöfe von Bonifatius bis Uriel von Gemmingen, 742?–1514. Vol. I, ed. Cornelius Will. Innsbruck, 1877.

Bondroit, A., "Les *precariae verbo regis* avant le concile de Leptinnes," *Revue d'histoire ecclésiastique*, I (1900), 41–60, 249–66, 430–47.

Boniface, St., Operum quae extant omnium pars prima-tertia. Migne, PL, Vol. LXXXIX.

Browne, George F., Boniface of Crediton and His Companions . . . London, 1910.

Dümmler, Ernst, S. Bonifatii et Lulli epistolae. Berlin, 1892. MGH, Epis. III (Epistolae Merovingici et Karolini aevi, Vol. I, No. VI).

Dünzelmann, E., Untersuchung über die ersten unter Karlmann und Pippin gehaltenen Concilien. Göttingen, 1869. Inaugural dissertation.

Fischer, Otto, Bonifatius, der Apostel der Deutschen, nach der Quellen dargestellt. Leipzig, 1881.

Flaskamp, Franz, "Das Bistum Erfurt," *Zeitschrift für vaterländische Geschichte und Altertumskunde*, Vol. LXXXIII (1925).

———— Das Hessen-Bistum Buraburg. Münster, 1927.

———— Das hessische Missionswerk des heilige Bonifatius. Duderstadt, 1926.

———— Die homiletische Wirksamkeit des heilige Bonifatius. Hildesheim, 1926.

———— Die Missionsmethode des heilige Bonifatius. Hildesheim, 1929.

Godard, Léon, "Quels sont les Africains que le pape Grégoire II défendit, en 723, d'élever au sacerdoce?" *Revue africaine*, V (1861), 48–53.

Hahn, Heinrich, Bonifaz und Lul; Ihre angelsächsischen Korrespondenten: Erzbischof Luls Leben. Leipzig, 1883.

Hahn, Heinrich, Jahrbücher des fränkischen Reichs, 741–752. Berlin, 1863. "Jahrbücher der deutschen Geschichte," Vol. III.

Hauck, Albert, Kirchengeschichte Deutschlands. 2d ed. Leipzig, 1898–1920.

Hefele, Karl J. von, Histoire des conciles, d'après les documents originaux. Tr., with critical notes, by Henri Leclercq. 10 vols. Paris, 1907–38.

Kuhlmann, Bernhard, Der heilige Bonifacius, Apostel der Deutschen. Paderborn, 1895.

Kurth, Godefroid, Saint Boniface (680–755). 3d ed. Paris, 1902.

Kylie, Edward, The English Correspondence of Saint Boniface; Being for the Most Part Letters Exchanged between the Apostle of the Germans and His English Friends. London, 1911.

Lau, Hermann, Die angelsächsische Missionsweise im Zeitalter des Bonifaz. Preetz, 1909. Inaugural dissertation.

Laux, Johann J., Der heilige Bonifatius, Apostel der Deutschen. Freiburg i. B., 1922.

Levinson, Wilhelm, Vitae S. Bonifatii archiepiscopi Moguntini. Hannover and Leipzig, 1905. "Scriptores rerum Germanicarum in usum scholarum."

Loening, Edgar, Geschichte des deutschen Kirchenrechts . . . 2 vols. Strassburg, 1878.

Loofs, Friedrich, Zur Chronologie der auf die fränkischen Synoden des hl. Bonifatius bezüglichen Briefe der bonifazischen Briefsammlung. Leipzig, 1881.

Nottarp, Hermann, Die Bistumserrichtung in Deutschland im 8. Jahrhundert. Stuttgart, 1920.

Oelsner, Ludwig. Jahrbücher des fränkischen Reiches unter König Pippin. Leipzig, 1871. "Jahrbücher der deutschen Geschichte," Vol. IV.

Pfahler, Georg, St. Bonifacius und seine Zeit. Regensburg, 1880.

Sägmüller, Johann B., Lehrbuch des katholischen Kirchenrechts. 3d ed., 2 vols. Freiburg i. B, 1914.

Schnürer, Gustav, Bonifatius: die Bekehrung der Deutschen zum Christentum. Mainz, 1909.

Schwahn, M. B., "S. Boniface et les missionaires de la Germanie au VIIIe siècle," La Science sociale, 1900–1902.

Spelman, Sir Henry, Concilia, decreta, leges, constitutiones, in re ecclesiarum orbis Britannici. 2 vols. London, 1639–64.

Tangl, Michael, Bonifatiusfragen. Berlin, 1919. "Abhandlungen der preussischen Akademie der Wissenschaften. Phil.-hist. Klasse," Jahrg. 1919, No. 2.

————— Die Briefe des heiligen Bonifatius und Lullus. Berlin, 1916.

————— Die Briefe des heiligen Bonifatius, nach der Ausgabe in den Monumenta Germaniae historica in Auswahl übersetzt und erläutert. Leipzig, 1912. "Die Geschichtschreiber der deutschen Vorzeit," 92.

————— "Studien zur Neuausgabe der Bonifatius-Briefe," *Neues Archiv der Gesellschaft für ältere deutsche Geschichtskunde*, XL (1916), 639–790, XLI (1917), 23–101.

Vacant, A., and E. Mangenot, eds., Dictionnaire de théologie catholique. Paris, 1909–

Vahle, Heinz, Die Widerstände gegen das Werk des Bonifatius . . . Emsdetten, 1934. Inaugural dissertation.

Werner, August, Bonifacius, der Apostel der Deutschen, und die Romanisierung von Mitteleuropa. Leipzig, 1875.

Willibald, St., bishop of Eichstadt, The Life of Saint Boniface . . . translated . . . by George W. Robinson. Cambridge, Mass., 1916.

Wissig, Otto, Iroschotten und Bonifatius in Deutschland. Gütersloh, 1932.

Index

CPSIA information can be obtained at www.ICGtesting.com
Printed in the USA
LVOW01*2150180614

390613LV00001BB/6/P